The Good Books Devotional

The

Good Books
Devotional
Volume I

by
D. Thaine Norris
Foreword by
Lengdung Tungchamma

WALKING TOGETHER PRESS
ESTES PARK · JENTA MANGORO

Published in 2023 by
Walking Together Press
Estes Park, Colorado USA
Jenta Mangoro, Jos, Plateau Nigeria
https://walkingtogether.press

In keeping with a book about public domain books, all Scripture quotations in this text are from the *World English Bible,* which is in the public domain.

ISBN: 978-1-961568-22-8

Cover design by D. Thaine Norris
Typeset in Adobe Garamond Pro by D. Thaine Norris

Contents

Acknowledgments

THIS book, along with the entire Scripture Testimony Collection, could not have happened without the wonderful intercontinental team at Walking Together Press, especially Lengdung Tungchamma, Peter Kurdor, and Jeremy Norris.

Special thanks to Eb Roell for taking me to Africa the first time, and then for being such an integral part of the beginnings of the Jenta Reads Community Library and Walking Together Press.

Thanks to Eb and to my wife, Erika Norris, for proofreading the manuscript, and to Erika for enduring months of seeing the back of my head.

And thank you Jesus, for living in and through Your servants, for being the cause of so many amazing stories, and for inspiring some of these servants to *write them down*.

Foreword

To be a Christian is to accept a tall order. When one accepts the invitation of Jesus, one accepts a very different way of life... a way that goes against the human way... a way that rejects human nature. The invitation of Jesus is an invitation to alter everything about ourselves.

But can we really live this way, against our instincts? I struggled with this challenge in the early days of my surrender to Christ. Did Jesus really mean it when he said we should turn the other cheek when someone slaps us? Did Jesus really mean it when he said we should love our neighbours as ourselves?

Christians have interpreted the words of Jesus in many different ways. Some have argued that he did not really mean what he said, he expected us to use "common sense" whenever confronted with a situation that requires us obey scriptural truth. By common sense they mean, when faced with a situation like that in the Parable of the Good Samaritan, we should ignore the wounded man because we are trying to run away from danger ourselves, or the injured man will die anyway, so any effort to save him is wasted effort. This is common sense to the human nature.

Some have said Jesus was not exactly serious about what he said. Surely he would sympathize with our human nature. While he teaches not look at a woman lustfully, he knows we are carnal and that it is perfectly natural to act that way.

However, the more I read the words of Jesus, the more I realize He was not joking. When Jesus said "...love your neighbor as yourself" (Mark 12:31), he meant it, literally. He said "Don't judge, and you won't be judged. Don't condemn, and you won't be condemned. Set free (forgive), and you will be set free (forgiven)." (Luke 6:37) This verse from Luke is highly relevant to me. By nature I am an excellent critic, and can condemn things easily; and there was one thing I could not forgive. My mother had died in a hospital while giving birth to my baby brother. It was mostly the incompetence of the hospital that led to the deaths of my brother and my mother. Did Jesus really mean I should forgive this? Yes, he did. But how can I forgive? Just like Jesus did.

Yes, *just like Jesus did.* Jesus did not merely leave us with a tall order. He also left us with an example, to show that his commands are doable. The world would not be changed by His teachings alone, the world needed an example, so He set the example. Of course, we can dismiss the example of Jesus by saying, "He was God, so it's all easy for him." We might say this about Jesus, but can we say the same about a Chinese believer who lost his parents, wife and children, and property to violent persecutors, then was empowered by the Spirit to forgive? (From *By My Spirit,* by Jonathan Goforth.) We can try to say it was easy for Jesus, but what do we do with Dr. Baedeker who left a comfortable and prosperous life in England, to spend the rest of his life ministering to the lowliest rejects of society in awful Siberian prisons? (From *Dr. Baedeker and His Apostolic Work in Russia,* by Robert Latimer.) These examples, and many more from the *Scripture Testimony Collection* shatter our excuses and provide us with inspiration.

If God can empower regular people like us to do these kinds of "tall order" things, then He can do that in me.

The reading of Christian biographies has been a total repudiation of the explanations some Christians have about the instructions of Jesus.

These biographies are full of ordinary men and women, many of them with deficiencies, just like the disciples, just like me, but they were able to take Jesus at his word and—by his power—his word proved true. The more I learned about these people, the more I was encouraged in my own Christian journey. I am not on a hopeless journey. It is a journey that many have taken and I hope you will take it too.

In this devotional, we have collected some of the best stories from the various books in the *Scripture Testimony Collection*. Stories are powerful. They provide insight, inspiration and clarity. These stories have blessed us, and we are confident that they will bless you too.

I am still a struggling Christian, but a struggling Christian who looks to Jesus as the Author and Finisher of my faith. Seeing the examples of Chinese believers, George Müller, Hudson Taylor, Sundar Singh, and many others, shows me that my struggles are not unique. Their triumphs inspire me to keep depending on God. I know this work he has started in me will be completed, because I see that his work was completed in *their* lives.

We hope that some of these books will move you to your knees and remind you to hold on to Biblical truth. We hope that some of them will move you closer to God, and that some of them will move you closer to living as the Bible instructs. We hope that some of these testimonies will keep you focused on the heavenly race, and that they will inspire you to live a life worthy of standing before God and hearing "Well done, good and faithful servant."

LENGDUNG TUNGCHAMMA
Co-Founder Jenta Reads Community Library
Jenta Mangoro, Jos, Nigeria

The Good Books Devotional

Chapter I

Introduction to the
Good Books Devotional

I N the summer of 2017 a group of young people in a slum community of Jos, Nigeria called Jenta started a library with the goal to #ChangeTheNarrative. Prior to the library, the area was known as the bad part of town. But in just a few years, Jenta would be widely known in Nigeria as the community with the Jenta Reads Community Library, inspiring spin-off libraries far and wide.

In May 2018 I had the opportunity to take books to this fledgling library, which at the time was merely a small room with two tables, each with a few stacks of books. Yet this was *the only public library* in a city of nearly a million people. But in their own amazing faith story, which is told at length elsewhere, God provided such that within the year Jenta Reads grew to have a three-room building, new book cases with thousands of books, tables, computers, a librarian, and a dedicated team of volunteers, led by two young men in their twenties, Philip Dimka and Lengdung Tungchamma.

One of the unexpected aspects of that first trip to Jenta was the importance of stories of faith. Morning and evening each day I spent sitting in the shade of a mango tree, while random youths would walk up and—without even a greeting—ask a question like, "Can you tell me how to walk more deeply with Jesus?" Hardly knowing where to begin, I would pray and trust the promise of Jesus in Luke 12:12 that, "the Holy Spirit will teach you in that very hour what you ought to say." Of course we would go to the Scriptures to learn from Jesus Himself, but invariably I would end up telling stories.

For example, Jesus teaches to "love your enemies and pray for those who persecute you." That's a beautiful statement, but who has actually done that? In a country plagued with crime and sectarian violence, this is a relevant question. At this point in the conversation I related the story of Corrie ten Boom receiving supernatural strength to forgive her former tormentor during World War II, a German prison guard at the Ravensbrück concentration camp.* Her story put to rest any notion that Jesus was merely saying pretty things. There is real power—because He is the real power—behind our living by faith. We can take Him at His word. We can trust Him implicitly.

After that 2018 book delivery, I started a website to collect more stories of faith, written in article-length stories. But then, upon learning that Lengdung has a degree in Computer Science, and with my own background in software engineering, we expanded on the faith-story idea and built a database of thousands of Christian biographies and spiritual testimonies, both by scanning books and by accessing public domain texts on the Internet. Then, using data science to analyze this database, we have been able to identify and categorize thousands of faith stories that empirically demonstrate the reality of God and the truth of His teachings. The entire project is summarized by the question, "Who has ever trusted God like that?" This database of categorized stories is called the *Scripture Testimony Index,* and is a freely available, forever-ad-free resource at https://walkingtogether.life.

---

* This amazing story is from another *must-read* book, *The Hiding Place* by Corrie ten Boom. Have you read it yet?

The very nature of data science is to discover trends and patterns in data, and over time it revealed some *really good* books, many of which we had never heard, and many in the public domain. This was the genesis of the *Scripture Testimony Collection* from Walking Together Press.

※

One evening, after finally receiving the last proof copies of the books in the Scripture Testimony Collection, giddy with excitement, I plopped them all down on the coffee table in front of our Friday evening Bible study. With a goofy grin on my face, I watched as people examined them. Their reactions were tepid at best. "Nice. These are pretty." Oh no! If only they knew what was in these books! One by one I began to explain who these people were and what their books are about, after which they were asking if they could take them home to read. It was that evening that I decided to write this book.

The Good Books Devotional

What kind of a title is "The Good Books Devotional?" If this book were written 150 years ago we might have titled this little volume, "The Devotional that Seeks to Introduce the Reader to an Indispensable Collection of Must-Read Titles from the Public Domain, Volume I," because that is what it seeks to do. But that title is just too long.

A book that is in the public domain means that it is old enough that the author has been deceased for, in most countries, seventy or more years, and therefore the copyright for the book has expired. Anyone is free to reproduce the work, and even profit from it. This has led to companies devoted to republishing free content. Sadly, many of these companies maximize quantity over quality, and can provide no other compelling reason to read one of these old books other than the fact that its mere existence is part of the "knowledge base of civilization." The eleven titles in the *Scripture Testimony*

Collection, Series I, are *really good* books that we have read over and over, and through which we have gained deep spiritual benefit.

These books mostly came to our attention through our data science work because each contains profound stories of faith. The process went something like this:

"Wow, what a cool story of answered prayer from Dr. Baedeker!"

"Who is Dr. Baedeker? Have you heard of him?"

"I haven't before now, but this book is amazing!"

And then some of these books, like *George Müller of Bristol, Hudson Taylor, Mimosa,* and *How I Know God Answers Prayer* are fairly well-known, and have already been formative in our lives, even playing roles in the founding of the Jenta Reads Community Library and in the formation of Walking Together Press.

Through relating actual experiences, each of these books testifies of the reality, love, and faithfulness of God, through answered prayer, miraculous transformation, and specific leading; and many times in ways we could never imagine.

Faith Beyond Imagination

In *The Magician's Nephew,* a fairy-tale by C. S. Lewis, there is a scene in which the characters in the story are present to witness the creation song that brings the land of Narnia into existence. One of these characters is a simple, hard-working, plain-spoken London cabby who is suddenly presented with things of wonder beyond his imagination. "Glory be!" said the Cabby. "I'd ha' been a better man all my life if I'd known there were things like this."

It's like that with stories of faith. Many of us simply are not aware that we can *dare* to trust God with our day-to-day lives. We are not aware of the heavenly richness of life experienced while metaphorically holding the hand of Jesus, who said that He came that we might have life, and have it *abundantly.* Reading the real-life stories of faith contained in books like these in the *Scripture Testimony Collection* opens our eyes to spiritual things of wonder beyond our imaginations. It is surely our hope in republishing these titles that these stories would further open our hearts to "...him who is able to do exceedingly abundantly above all that we ask or think, according to the power that works in us" (Ephesians 3:20)

With a few exceptions, the people in these books are not household names, even in missionary-minded Christian circles, and yet they have not only had rich experiences of walking with God, they have written beautifully about them for the dual purposes of bringing glory to God and encouraging others. I think all of us face the problem of trying to convince a friend to read a good book they have never heard of before. This daily devotional is intended both to draw out powerful spiritual lessons from real-life stories, and as a way for us at Walking Together Press to say, "What? You have never heard of this book? Here, let me read you this short excerpt..."

A Devotional

This book serves a two-fold purpose; to introduce these good books to the reader so that it might be understood why they are still worth reading after a hundred years, and to provide a few "short excerpts" with some spiritual application to prove the point. Each chapter introduces a book from the *Scripture Testimony Collection,* and then is followed by two or three devotions.

From time to time the narrative slips into the first person as I share from my own experiences. Many of these amazing stories have aided in my own spiritual formation, as well as providing illustrations for teaching in different contexts.

D. THAINE NORRIS
Editor
Walking Together Press

Chapter II

George Müller of Bristol

Imagine a man walking into a poor rural village containing thousands of people and then promising to take care of their every need; food, clothing, housing, education. And then imagine that he proposed to do this without telling anyone other than God that these needs even existed. This man was George Müller, and that village was the more than ten thousand orphans for whom he cared, over sixty years of his life.

In his youth, George Müller was such a slave to money that he would lie, cheat, and steal to get it. But then God set him free. He said, "There was a day when I died, utterly died...died to George Müller, his opinions, preferences, tastes and will—died to the world, its approval or censure—died to the approval or blame even of my brethren and friends..." God transformed this wayward youth into a humble man of faith who set about—as one of his primary life goals—to prove to the world that God is alive, that He loves us, and that He is trustworthy and faithful. In spite of his indifference to money, or perhaps because of it, God allowed more than £1,300,000*

---

* £1,300,000 in 1898 is worth about £140,000,000, or $172,000,000 in 2023

to pass through his hands towards the needs and support of orphans, missionaries, schools, evangelism, and more. In order to provide the world with hard evidence, Müller meticulously recorded every day's provision in an annually refreshed publication called *The Narrative of the Lord's Dealings with George Müller.* Written to the glory of God the Provider with accountant-like precision, it is a necessarily tedious document, showing the utter consistency and dependability of our faithful Heavenly Father, never letting His children go without their daily bread.

George Müller desired to bring glory to God and to inspire others through his life of trust, and God profoundly honored this desire. In Müller's lifetime, he was able to visit orphanages in Holland and Japan, each started and run by faith, and inspired by reading his *Narrative.* In the late 1850's, a young Irishman read George Müller's *Narrative* and boldly declared that he would *dare* to trust God, "like Mr. Müller." This was the starting point for one of the most widespread revivals in history, sweeping from Ireland through England, Wales, and Scotland. Today in the twenty-first century there are nearly 200 million Chinese believers that were directly or indirectly influenced by George Müller's example to, and financial support of, Hudson Taylor and the China Inland Mission. Even our own Jenta Reads Community Library, mentioned in the previous chapter, was inspired by George Müller's life of simple trust. The people featured in *every* book of the *Scripture Testimony Collection,* no matter what culture they are from, were either directly or indirectly influenced by his life. God's impact through this humble servant simply cannot be quantified this side of heaven. Perhaps this is a glimpse of the "greater things" that Jesus promised in John 14:12.

First published in 1899, the year after Müller's death, *George Müller of Bristol* was the first authorized biography. It was written by Müller's American friend Arthur T. Pierson, author of numerous books on missions, theology, apologetics, and biography, and who was also a pastor, including two years over Charles Spurgeon's church in London. While Müller's own *Narrative* is powerful, he rarely talks about himself. Pierson skillfully draws deep spiritual lessons from Müller's life, combining the *Narrative's* testimonies of God's provision and faithfulness with their effect on Müller and others, which makes this biography one of the most important Christian books of all time. And that is not a hyperbolic statement. If you haven't already, you simply *must* read it.

Following are three Scriptural devotions drawn from passages in the book, *George Müller of Bristol.*

Devotion 1: Depending Solely Upon God

WHILE ultimately an astonishing amount of money passed through Mr. Müller's hands, the reality was that most of those funds came on a day-to-day, as-needed basis, as can be seen by the following story.

In the autumn of 1841 it pleased God that, beyond any previous period, there should be a severe test of faith. For some months the supplies had been comparatively abundant, but now, from day to day and from meal to meal, the eye of faith had to be turned to the Lord, and, notwithstanding continuance in prayer, help seemed at times to fail, so much so that it was a special sign of God's grace that, during this long trial of delay, the confidence of Mr. Müller and his helpers did not altogether give way. But he and they were held up, and he unwaveringly rested on the fatherly pity of God.

On one occasion a poor woman gave two pence, adding, "It is but a trifle, but I must give it to you." Yet so opportune was the gift of these 'two mites' that one of these two pence was just what was at that time needed to make up the sum required to buy bread for immediate use. At another time eight pence more being necessary to provide for the next meal, but seven pence were in hand; but on opening one of the boxes, one penny only was found deposited, and thus a single penny was traced to the Father's care.

But then Mr. Müller was prompted to go a step further in his *sole* dependence upon God. While he never openly engaged in fundraising, it was true that the annual publication of *The Narrative* raised public awareness of the work, which could lead to more donations. Consequently here is what he did:

It was in December of this same year, 1841, that, in order to show how solely dependence was placed on a heavenly Provider, it was determined to delay for a while both the holding of any public meeting and the printing of the Annual Report. Mr. Müller was confident that, though no word should be either spoken or printed about the work and its needs, the means would still be supplied. As a matter of fact the report of 1841-2 was thus postponed for five months; and so, in the midst of deep poverty and partly because of the very pressure of such need, another bold step was taken, which, like the cutting away of the ropes that held the life-boat, in that Mediterranean shipwreck [Acts 27:32], threw Mr. Müller, and all that were with him in the work, more completely on the promise and the providence of God.

It might be inferred that, where such a decision was made, the Lord would make haste to reward at once such courageous confidence. And yet, so mysterious are His ways, that never, up to that time, had Mr. Müller's faith been tried so sharply as between December 12, 1841, and April 12, 1842. During these four months, again, it was as though God were saying, "I will now see whether indeed you truly lean on Me and look to Me." At any time during this trial, Mr. Müller might have changed his course, holding the public meeting and publishing the report, for, outside the few who were in his councils, no one knew of the determination, and in fact many children of God, looking for the usual year's journal of 'The Lord's Dealings,' were surprised at the delay. But the conclusion conscientiously reached was, for the glory of the Lord, as steadfastly pursued, and again Jehovah Jireh revealed His faithfulness.

During this four months, on March 9, 1842, the need was so extreme that, had no help come, the work could not have gone on. But, on that day, from a brother living near Dublin, ten pounds came: and the hand of the Lord clearly appeared in this gift, for when the post had already come and no letter had come with it, there was a strong confidence suggested to Mr. Müller's mind that deliverance was at hand; and so it proved, for presently the letter was brought to him, having been delivered at one of the other houses. During this same month, it was necessary once to delay dinner for about a half-hour, because of a lack of supplies. Such a postponement had scarcely ever been known before, and very rarely was it repeated in the entire after-history of the work, though thousands of mouths had to be daily fed.

Theme

God provides exactly what is needed
PHILIPPIANS 4:19:
My God will supply every need of yours according to his riches in glory in Christ Jesus.
2 CORINTHIANS 8:15:
As it is written, "He who gathered much had nothing left over, and he who gathered little had no lack."

Devotion

Charles Dickens wrote about George Müller in 1857 that "he believes, with a liveliness of faith perhaps unequaled in our time, that all things fitting for His children will be supplied by our Father in heaven in direct answer to trustful prayer." Dickens was skeptical of Müller's theological views, but he concluded the introduction to his lengthy article by saying, "Trusting in prayer only, he never starved, and has obtained more than a hundred thousand pounds for pious uses."*

Charles Dickens respectfully tells George Müller's life story, letting the incredible facts speak for themselves, but it is clear that he finds the idea of trusting God for every little thing hard to grasp. To the average person, it seems ridiculous to not know how tomorrow's needs, or even the next hour's needs will be met. We want security. We want to know that money will always be there. We want to win the lottery and never have to worry about money again.

That is the point. George Müller made it his life mission to demonstrate that true security is not having an endless supply of money, but is only found in the One who provides our *daily* bread. God's provision is not even about money, it's about relationship.

Let's conduct a thought experiment...

According to the Bank of England Inflation Calculator, £1,300,000 of 1898 money is worth about £140,000,000 (about $172,000,000) in 2023. What if, when George Müller decided to trust God for all his needs and first asked for provision, God had simply given him the entire sum needed for his lifetime? What could be wrong with that? Isn't that the logical end of what we are seeking in "financial security?"

There is so much wrong with this fictitious scenario. Would the previously money-obsessed Müller be ruined by such an enormous sum? How would he know how such sums were supposed to be spent, not knowing the future needs? Would the orphanage work have naturally grown out of such a windfall? Questions abound. But the worst result would be that, having all the money he would *ever* need, he would never *need* to ask God again. We humans are prone to forgetfulness (witness the Israelites in the wilderness), so it would be easy to imagine that in time "rich Müller" would forget where it all came from.

---

*   Dickens, Charles. 1850. *Household Words.* London: Bradbury & Evans. No. 398. November 7, 1857.

Relationship begins with dependence. None of us is self-sufficient. Even the simplest friendship is a dependence upon what the other person brings to the relationship. Therefore a relationship with God begins with the humility of dependence—the asking—and then, through provision, is built up through thanksgiving. And it is His delight to give us what is good! (Matthew 7:11)

The stories from George Müller's life quoted earlier show part of the ongoing process of his learning how to trust God for every little thing, from a penny to thousands of pounds, and how God delighted to give exactly what was needed, exactly when it was needed. Why worry about any need when God always provided? This is true security.

Reflection

Living by faith is profoundly exciting. Not only do we see the reality and loving character of God as He provides, but we have an assurance that we are in His will. George Müller was not asking for riches for himself, instead, as a co-laborer with God, he was trusting Him to supply all that was needed for the Kingdom mission.

Perhaps God is calling you to participate in some great Kingdom work, but you have no idea how it would be paid for. Humbly trust Him, like George Müller!

⁜

This story begins on page 113 of the Scripture Testimony Edition of *George Müller of Bristol* from Walking Together Press.

Devotion 2: *The Answer is Yet to Come*

WHILE taking tea at the home of a Christian sister in 1835, George Müller was reacquainted with a book that had already been a profound influence on him, the biography of fellow countryman, August H. Francké of Halle, Germany. Nearly one hundred fifty years earlier, Francké had established a large orphan house which was funded by faith alone. Müller was inspired by this, and was encouraged to undertake a similar work, and by similar means. (Incidentally, in later years George Müller's own writings would serve as inspirations for many other great Kingdom works of faith.)

> ...on December 2, 1835, the first formal step was taken in ordering printed bills announcing a public meeting for the week following, when the proposal to open an orphan house was to be laid before brethren, and further light to be sought unitedly as to the mind of the Lord.
>
> Three days later, in reading the Psalms, he was struck with these nine words:
>
> *"Open thy mouth wide, and I will fill it." (Psalm 81:10)*

From that moment this text formed one of his great life-mottoes, and this promise became a power in moulding all his work. Hitherto he had not prayed for the supply of money or of helpers, but he was now led to apply this scripture confidently to this new plan, and at once *boldly to ask for premises, and for one thousand pounds in money, and for suitable helpers to take charge of the children.* Two days after, he received, in furtherance of his work, the first gift of money—one shilling—and within two days more the first donation in furniture—a large wardrobe.

One by one, Müller's bold requests of God were fulfilled, even people willing to give themselves to the work, as seen in a letter from a brother and sister.

"We propose ourselves for the service of the intended orphan house, if you think us qualified for it; also to give up all the furniture, etc., which the Lord has given us, for its use; and to do this without receiving any salary whatever; believing that, if it be the will of the Lord to employ us, He will supply all our need."

God had provided everything, buildings, people, furniture, and funds to support it all. But Mr. Müller had boldly asked for one thousand pounds in money, and was still expecting its arrival.

The founder of this orphan work, who had at the first asked for one thousand pounds of God, tells us that, in his own mind, the thing was *as good as done,* so that he often gave thanks for this large sum as though already in hand. (Mark 11:24; 1 John 5:14, 15) This habit of counting a promise as fulfilled had much to do with the triumphs of his faith and the success of his labour. Now that the first part of his *Narrative of the Lord's Dealings* was about to issue from the press, he felt that it would much honour the Master whom he served *if the entire amount should be actually in hand before the Narrative should appear, and without any one having been asked to contribute.* He therefore gave himself anew to prayer; and on June 15th the whole sum was complete, no appeal having been made but to the Living God, before whom, as he records with his usual mathematical precision, he had daily brought his petition for *eighteen months and ten days.*

Theme

Whatever you ask in prayer, in faith, abiding, you will receive
    MATTHEW 21:22
        All things, whatever you ask in prayer, believing, you will receive.
    MARK 11:24
        Therefore I tell you, all things whatever you pray and ask for, *believe that you have received them,* and you shall have them. (emphasis added)
    JOHN 15:7
        If you remain in me, and my words remain in you, you will ask whatever you desire, and it will be done for you.
    1 JOHN 5:14-15
        This is the boldness which we have toward him, that if we ask anything according to his will, he listens to us. And if we know that he listens to us, whatever we ask, we know that we have the petitions which we have asked of him.

Devotion

In our increasingly digital society with instant transactions, the term, "The check's in the mail," is becoming less and less familiar. But the idea still holds true that we are put at ease—and are excited—knowing that money will soon be here. Why? Because the sender of the funds said so. The money is not yet in hand, but we are at ease, trusting in the character of the sender. We might even contact this person and say "thank you" before the funds actually arrive.

In the same way, God has promised in His word to give us what we ask. If a human being can be trusted to send funds merely because he said so, then how much more can we trust the Living God to keep His plain-spoken promises? George Müller was so convinced of both the character of his Heavenly Father, and that he was walking in the Divine Will, that he boldly gave thanks for things before they were actually in hand.

What is required for this kind of faith?

Hebrews 11:6 says, "Without faith it is impossible to be well pleasing to him, for he who comes to God must believe that *he exists, and that he is a rewarder of those who seek him.*" It's as simple as that. George Müller believed that God exists, and that His character is such that He means what He says.

The overarching purpose of George Müller's life was to demonstrate to the world that not only does God *exist,* but that He is ever present and ready for us to join Him in the exciting and fulfilling work of His Kingdom. And most of all, that God—though invisible—is far more trustworthy and willing to send what we need, than any person we may see face to face.

Reflection

Heavenly Father, as we pray "Thy Kingdom come," show us what you are doing and how we can be a part of it. Then, knowing we are in your will, help us to simply ask for the things that are needed to accomplish the task, and to give thanks in advance of the arrival of those things.

This story begins on page 76 of the Scripture Testimony Edition of *George Müller of Bristol* from Walking Together Press.

Devotion 3: Working with God

G EORGE Müller published his *Narrative of the Lord's Dealings* primarily to demonstrate the reality and faithfulness of God by meticulously recording every penny he received as a result of prayer alone. Largely an accounting ledger, the book is, by design, tedious to read. However, from time to time Müller shares genuine nuggets of wisdom that he has learned through his life of trust, such as the following:

April 21. I would offer here a word of warning to believers. Often the work of the Lord itself may be a temptation to keep us from that communion with him which is so essential to the benefit of our own souls. On the 19th I had left Dartmouth, conversed a good deal that day, preached in the evening, walked afterwards eight miles, had only about five hours' sleep, travelled again the next day twenty-five miles, preached twice, and conversed very much besides, went to bed at eleven, and arose before five. All this shows that my body and spirit required rest, and, therefore, however careless about the Lord's work I might have appeared to my brethren, I ought to have had a great deal of quiet time for prayer and reading the word, especially as I had a long journey before me that day, and as I was going to Bristol, which in itself required much prayer. Instead of this, I hurried to the prayer meeting, after a few minutes' private prayer. But let none think that public prayer will make up for closet communion. Then again, afterwards, when I ought to have withdrawn myself, as it were, by force, from the company of beloved brethren and sisters, and given my testimony for the Lord, (and, indeed, it would have been the best testimony I could have given them,) by telling them that I needed secret communion with the Lord, I did not do so, but spent the time, till the coach came, in conversation with them. Now, however profitable in some respects it may have been made to those with whom I was on that morning, yet my own soul needed food; and not having had it, I was lean, and felt the effects of it the whole day; and hence I believe it came that I was dumb on the coach, and did not speak a word for Christ, nor give away a single tract, though I had my pockets full on purpose.*

Theme

Like Jesus, the believer needs time alone with God
MARK 1:35
> Early in the morning, while it was still dark, he rose up and went out, and departed into a deserted place, and prayed there.
LUKE 5:15-16
> But the report concerning him spread much more, and great multitudes came together to hear, and to be healed by him of their infirmities. But he withdrew himself into the desert, and prayed.

Devotion

In the following passage from the book *George Müller of Bristol,* author and pastor Arthur T. Pierson unpacks a beautiful devotional lesson for us from this early ministry experience of George Müller.

---

* Müller, George, and Herman Lincoln Wayland. 1868. *The Life of Trust: Being A Narrative of the Lord's Dealings with George Müller.* Boston, Gould and Lincoln; New York, Sheldon and company; [etc., etc.]. pg. 82

On April 20th Mr. Müller left for Bristol. On the journey he was dumb, having no liberty in speaking for Christ or even in giving away tracts, and this led him to reflect. He saw that the so-called 'work of the Lord' had tempted him to substitute action for meditation and communion. He had neglected that still hour with God which supplies to spiritual life alike its breath and its bread. No lesson is more important for us to learn, yet how slow are we to learn it: that for the lack of habitual seasons set apart for devout meditation upon the word of God and for prayer, nothing else will compensate....

Here Mr. Müller had the grace to detect one of the foremost perils of a busy man in this day of insane hurry. *He saw that if we are to feed others we must be fed;* and that even public and united exercises of praise and prayer can never supply that food which is dealt out to the believer only in the closet—the shut-in place with its closed door and open window, where he meets God alone.

...In the word of God we find a divine prescription for a true prosperity. God says to Joshua, "This book of the law shall not depart out of thy mouth; but thou shalt meditate therein day and night, that thou mayest observe to do according to all that is written therein: for then thou shalt make thy way prosperous, and then thou shalt have good success" (Joshua 1:8)

Five hundred years later the inspired author of the first Psalm repeats the promise in unmistakable terms. The Spirit there says of him whose delight is in the law of the Lord and who in His law doth meditate day and night, that "he shall be like a tree planted by the rivers of water, that bringeth forth his fruit in his season; his leaf also shall not wither; and whatsoever he doeth shall prosper." Here the devout meditative student of the blessed book of God is likened to an evergreen tree planted beside unfailing supplies of moisture; his fruit is perennial, and so is his verdure—and whatsoever he doeth prospers!

More than a thousand years pass away, and, before the New Testament is sealed up as complete, once more the Spirit bears essentially the same blessed witness. "Whoso looketh into the perfect law of liberty and continueth" (i.e. continueth looking—meditating on what he there beholds, lest he forget the impression received through the mirror of the Word), "this man shall be blessed in his deed" (James 1:25)

Here then we have a threefold witness to the secret of true prosperity and unmingled blessing: devout meditation and reflection upon the Scriptures, which are at once a book of law, a river of life, and a mirror of self—fitted to convey the will of God, the life of God, and the transforming power of God. That believer makes a fatal mistake who for any cause neglects the prayerful study of the word of God. To read God's holy book, by it search one's self, and turn it into prayer and so into holy living, is the one great secret of growth in grace and godliness.

The worker for God must first be a worker with God: he must have power with God and must prevail with Him in prayer, if he is to have power with men and prevail with men in preaching or in any form of witnessing and serving. At all costs let us make sure of that highest preparation for our work—the preparation of our own souls; and for this we must take time to be alone with His word and His Spirit, that we may truly meet God, and understand His will and the revelation of Himself.

Reflection

If we are to feed others we must be fed.

The worker for God must first be a worker with God.

✵

This devotional excerpt from Dr. Arthur T. Pierson begins on page 55 of the Scripture Testimony Edition of *George Müller of Bristol* from Walking Together Press.

Chapter III

Dr. Baedeker and His Apostolic Work in Russia

D R. Frederick Baedeker, born in Germany in 1823, earned a doctorate in philosophy, became a successful business man and educator, then founded an elite prep school in Weston-super-Mare, England, to where he emigrated, married, and settled into a prosperous life. But at age forty-three, Dr. Baedeker attended a series of evangelistic meetings about which he said, "I went in a proud German infidel, and came out a humble, believing disciple of the Lord Jesus Christ."

God had specially prepared Dr. Baedeker through his former life of prosperity and influence to accomplish the ministry that would define the rest of his life. Through aristocratic connections, God granted Dr. Baedeker unprecedented access to the horrible prisons of Czarist Russia. At one point eighty-six-year-old George Müller laid his hands on Dr. Baedeker's head and "separated him to the special ministry to the banished brethren, committing him to the loving care of our Heavenly Father."

Unlike George Müller, who had to be delivered from a love of money, Dr. Baedeker was more like the rich young ruler Jesus encountered in

Luke 18:18-30, except that Dr. Baedeker did not go away sad (verse 23). Instead of enjoying the comforts of his upper-class position, Dr. Baedeker *joyfully* chose to spend his days and his personal wealth to visit the downcast and forgotten so that he might lift their chins with the hope of the glorious Gospel. At one point a skeptical customs official was won over when he learned that Dr. Baedeker was not only bringing Bibles to freely give away, but that he had purchased them "out of his own private purse." On another occasion, Dr. Baedeker was on a ship crowded with poor, hungry refugees, so he paid for the ship's kitchen to make a hearty meal for more than 500 people. Beautiful things like this contributed to Dr. Baedeker's ever-increasing and highly-visible sense of joy, along with a genuine affection for others that broke down the highest of walls in the hearts of the hardest of criminals.

Frequently in great need or danger, or facing opposition, Dr. Baedeker sought and found deliverance through prayer. These proofs of God's love and faithfulness are chronicled in story after story in this powerful biography. Originally published in 1907, the year after Dr. Baedeker's death, *Dr. Baedeker and His Apostolic Work in Russia* is an essential Christian biography. From the author, "A life-work so signally exemplary in its long-sustained heroism for Christ, and so rich in spiritual stimulus, could not be allowed to pass unchronicled." But from us at Walking Together Press, you simply *must* read this book. It will bless you profoundly.

Following are two Scriptural devotions drawn from passages in the book, *Dr. Baedeker and His Apostolic Work in Russia*.

Devotion 4: Jesus, Friend of Sinners and Outcasts

MORE than merely having permission to work in the prisons, Dr. Baedeker carried the tender heart of his Master, such that the prisoners were attracted to Jesus through him. This was illustrated by the following story from a time when Dr. Baedeker was doing prison ministry in Finland.

To write the story of Dr. Baedeker in Finland is to tell of the earlier years of the work of the Baroness Mathilda von Wrede. To her was given the honour of taking the doctor inside the gates of a Finnish prison for the first time. That first visit was made to the prison at Helsingfors [Helsinki] on the 3rd June 1887. On his subsequent visits the young Baroness was his faithful helper and interpreter....

University professors frequently interpreted for the doctor. On one occasion when a professor was translating, the convicts stood in their ranks respectfully listening, a set, stony look upon their faces. It was plain that they were quite unmoved. On his next visit to the same place the doctor was accompanied by the Baroness. He had not proceeded far with his address before the moist eyes of the listeners, and the convulsive twitching of their features, told him that the "arrows were sharp in the heart of the King's enemies."

"How was it?" he afterwards inquired wonderingly of one of the officers in attendance. "My former appeal they heard with indifference, and even resentment. Today the Word has found their consciences and hearts. Where lay the difference?"

The prison-officer's reply was significant:

"The difference, sir, was in the translation. When you said 'My beloved friends,' or 'My brothers,' your clever professor invariably translated the expressions 'men,' 'prisoners.' But the young lady translated it into Finnish as you expressed it in German: 'My beloved friends,' and 'My brothers.' The key that opened their hearts was human compassion and affection. They are not used to it.

Theme

Jesus came for sinners and those rejected by society

MATTHEW 8:1-13

"When he came down from the mountain, great multitudes followed him. Behold, a leper came to him and worshiped him, saying, 'Lord, if you want to, you can make me clean.' Jesus stretched out his hand and *touched* him, saying, 'I want to. Be made clean.' Immediately his leprosy was cleansed." (Matthew 8:1-3, emphasis added)

"When he came into Capernaum, a centurion came to him, asking him for help, saying, 'Lord, my servant lies in the house paralyzed, grievously tormented.' Jesus said to him, *'I will come and heal him.'*" (Matthew 8:5-7 emphasis added)

MATTHEW 26:6

"Now when Jesus was in Bethany, *in the house of Simon the leper...*" (emphasis added)

LUKE 5:30

"Their scribes and the Pharisees murmured against his disciples, saying, *'Why do you eat and drink with the tax collectors and sinners?'*" (emphasis added)

LUKE 7:34

> "The Son of Man has come eating and drinking, and you say, 'Behold, a gluttonous man, and a drunkard; *a friend of tax collectors and sinners!*'" (emphasis added)

Devotion

By his choices of words and manner of speaking, Dr. Baedeker acknowledged the dignity and humanity of those who had been cast off and rejected from society. This is the heart of God. It is not hard to imagine the reaction—the "moist eyes" and "convulsive twitching"—that resulted when Jesus likewise esteemed the cast-offs of society; Gentiles, lepers, sinners. He was *willing*. He *touched* them. He *ate* with them. He was their "beloved friend."

Is there someone in your life, perhaps a mentally handicapped person in your church, that simply craves the recognition of his or her dignity and equality in the eyes of God? Also consider the places in our society where we try to hide from view those who are hard to be around such as prisons, homeless shelters or camps, and nursing homes.

Esteem them. Visit them. Look at them. Smile at them. Talk to them. Pray with them.

Then perhaps one will ask, like Dr. Baedeker was frequently asked, "Why do you take your time to visit people like me?" at which point you can give an account of the hope that is in you. (1 Peter 3:15)

Reflection

Heavenly Father, open my eyes to the marginalized. Fill my heart with your love and compassion. Open the door for me to be a channel of that love to someone who needs it. Amen.

⁂

This story begins on page 151 of the Scripture Testimony Edition of *Dr. Baedeker and His Apostolic Work in Russia* from Walking Together Press.

Devotion 5: Under the Shadow of Thy Wing

THE following story, to which was alluded in the Introduction, is how the excellent book, *Dr. Baedeker and His Apostolic Work in Russia,* came to our attention.

The doctor [Dr. Baedeker] used to tell a story of an adventure that befell him on one of his visits to Transcaucasia. He had gone to conduct a series of meetings in a remote Armenian village among the mountains. It was in the end of December. The lateness of the season, the awful loneliness of the district, the risks of sudden snow-storms blinding the venturesome travellers, and covering tracks and way marks, all united to make the enterprise unattractive to those who knew the country. But the villagers had pressed him to visit them on so many previous occasions, when it was impossible for him to do so, that he could no longer resist their importunities.

On a memorable Christmas morning he bade them farewell, and with his Armenian interpreter and guide began the return journey. A few of the Christian brethren of the village accompanied them a little way to point out the track. Presently these also were left behind, and the two proceeded on their way alone.

How long they had been wandering in the wide solitudes before the guide became apprehensive that he had lost his bearings, I cannot remember hearing. The signs of night oncoming were beginning to appear—and when night falls, it falls suddenly in those regions—when the Armenian at length stood still and said:

"I can go no farther. I am spent. We have lost our way: and we are walking in vain!"

"Is there nothing you can recognise? Nothing to show us our where-abouts, or the direction we should take?" the doctor inquired.

"I have been seeking and watching for some sign or mark in Vain! Alas! We shall perish here of cold before the morning comes. The sun will set in a few minutes."

"Then let us just kneel down where we are and tell our Heavenly Father about it."

"Alas! that I was so foolish as to venture on such a journey, so unfamiliar, and at such a season!"

"God can take care of us and direct us. We will pray about it."

"Most likely we are many hours' journey from a human habitation, and my limbs are very weary. I shall never see my home again!"

"If you don't know the way, God does. Come, cease lamenting, and we will pray together."

The two men knelt silently side by side for a few minutes, Then the doctor turned his face to heaven, and prayed in his glad familiar manner to Him in Whom he trusted with such triumphant faith.

"Father, we cannot be lost, for we are in Thy hand all the time, and under the shadow of Thy wing. Thou knowest the way that we take. Send us help in our need, and guide us to safety!"

The prayer was interrupted by the distant barking of a dog.

"Listen! There is our Father's answer," said the doctor. "Praise His name, He hears, and does not keep us in suspense."

The welcome sound inspired the fainting guide with new strength. They turned in the direction of the sound, and following it, arrived as the night was closing in upon them, at a small Tartar encampment.

The surprise of the Tartars on seeing the new arrivals was very great.

"How did you come this way?" they inquired. "We never see travellers hereabouts in December. Are you not afraid of the snows?"

"My Master, who guided me here, can control the snows so that they shall not hurt us; and you can see He has done so, for no snow has fallen."

"Who is your Master, then?"

"Herr Jesus!"

And there and then he opened his mouth and began and preached unto them Jesus. Although they were Mohammedans they listened attentively to their venerable visitor, who afterwards told how they gave him and his guide the best entertainment in their power. His Christmas dinner that evening consisted of a piece of the common hard black bread, eaten by the Tartars, and a pomegranate! Writing home to his wife on the following day he told her he imagined the feastings in England; and was certain that nobody at home ate their Christmas dinner with more gratitude and joy in the Lord, than he ate his. In the morning, with much good will, the Tartars sent one of their number along with them to put them into the right road.

Theme

Don't be anxious, instead make requests known to God
PHILIPPIANS 4:6

Rejoice in the Lord always! Again I will say, "Rejoice!" Let your gentleness be known to all men. The Lord is at hand. In nothing be anxious, but in everything, by prayer and petition with thanksgiving, let your requests be made known to God. And the peace of God, which surpasses all understanding, will guard your hearts and your thoughts in Christ Jesus. (Philippians 4:4-7)

God answers prayer
JOHN 15:7
> If you remain in me, and my words remain in you, you will ask whatever you desire, and it will be done for you.

Devotion

Peace and anxiety are nearly perfect opposites, and so were the responses of Dr. Baedeker and his companion to their predicament. The Doctor's first reaction was to pray, and one can see expectancy, perhaps even excitement, in his repeated simple proposal. "Then let us just kneel down where we are and tell our Heavenly Father about it."

George Müller, one of Dr. Baedeker's personal mentors, took a sort of pleasure in hindrances, since they provided new opportunities for God to show His power. He said, "I had a secret satisfaction in the greatness of the difficulties which were in the way. So far from being cast down on account of them, they delighted my soul; for I only desired to do the will of the Lord in this matter."* This is what it looks like to rejoice in the Lord always, and in nothing be anxious. Why? Because the Lord is at hand!

With characteristic gentleness, the Doctor finally convinced his anxious friend to go to prayer "If you don't know the way, God does (the Lord is at hand). Come, cease lamenting (don't be anxious), and we will pray together (make our request known to God)."

Of course their speedy deliverance brought an inexplicable peace to the previously anxious companion. But surely Dr. Baedeker was able to so quickly and easily turn to prayer because he knew both from the promises of God and from empirical evidence, that he could "ask whatsoever ye will, and it shall be done unto you." Jesus does not make this promise as an "Oh, by the way..." statement. He is emphatic.

---

* Pierson, Arthur T. 2023. *George Müller of Bristol (Scripture Testimony Edition)*. Estes Park: Walking Together Press. pg. 118

In His continuous discourse to the disciples recorded in the Gospel of John, Jesus tells them, and those who would follow them (John 17:20), to ask the Father... seven times! (John 14:13, 14; John 15:7, 16; John 16:23, 24, 26)

Reflection

The promises of God are true. As we rely on Him again and again, we will come to a place of saying about every new difficulty, "I am excited to see how God works this one out!"

⁂

This story begins on page 49 of the Scripture Testimony Edition of *Dr. Baedeker and His Apostolic Work in Russia* from Walking Together Press.

Personal Story

On the last day of my first visit to Nigeria, the book-delivery trip mentioned in the Introduction, we were traveling by car from Jos, home of the Jenta Reads Community Library, to the airport in Abuja, the capital city. The trip is about four hours on treacherous roads full of potholes and police checkpoints. At one of these checkpoints, our driver got into an argument with the police over his paperwork. The driver was standing outside his open car door, toe to toe with a young officer, eyes flashing. My friend Philip had exited the passenger side and was meekly approaching to see if he could help. I was in the back seat with Lengdung and more friends. Suddenly, a senior officer came over and dove behind the driver and into the driver's seat, closed the door, started the engine, and drove off with us in the car, leaving the driver and Philip behind!

Up to this point, the trip had been so full of blessing, and so clearly led by the Holy Spirit, that my first response was, "Well, I am excited to see how God gets us out of this situation!" It seems strange as I write it now, but I don't think I have ever experienced such perfect peace as I did in those moments.

We drove for a while through a small village, then stopped at a humble police station, where we all got out and just stood around, waiting. Nobody spoke to us, nor would anyone answer our questions, as if we didn't even exist. Apparently the driver's passengers were not their problem. But, like Dr. Baedeker experienced in the waning light of a winter night in the forest, I had peace and confidence in our Father that He was caring for us, and that we would make it to the airport in time. And like George Müller, I was excited to see how He would work it out, *because I knew He would!* Sure enough, in half an hour or so, the driver and Philip arrived on motorcycles. Somehow, unknown to us, the conflict had been resolved, and we were soon on our way.

Chapter IV

Recollections of an Evangelist

ROBERT Gribble was a simple, uneducated man, whom God uniquely prepared to work with simple, uneducated farmers and laborers who lived in the villages of the bucolic Devonshire countryside. There are parallels between that time and place, and our own. Perhaps surprising to a modern reader, rural Britain in the first part of the nineteenth century was an area unreached with the Gospel. In spite of the long presence of the established church, most people had never even heard the name of Jesus, or if they had, they did not know that He is able to save and to transform souls. Robert Gribble worked with people in a post-Christian time much like our own.

The life story of Robert Gribble as told in his *Recollections of an Evangelist* may seem quaint, or even sentimental, to the modern reader. But it is not hard to see that the opposition to the Gospel of that time is not so different from its opposition in our time. If that is true, then perhaps there is something for the modern to learn from the simple faith and persistent prayer of the Kingdom workers in Gribble's time. Their methods were simple. For example, one of Gribble's co-laborers felt led to start a prayer meeting in his community. When his neighbors told him no one would come, he said, "Then I will hold one by myself." God rewarded this attitude with great fruit. This and similar stories in the book are refreshing to the soul, and inspiring. Gribble himself would follow the leading of the Holy Spirit to move to a new community and live as a good neighbor for several years, while seeking opportunities to preach the glad tidings of the Good News. In time, a church would be planted and established, and Gribble would follow the Spirit to the next place. George Müller joined Gribble in the work, and was a guest preacher in some of these places.

What would happen if we trusted God and humbly sought Him for the sake of our neighbors in our own time and place? Pete Greig, British pastor, author, speaker, and one of the founders of the 24/7 prayer movement, in his 2016 book, *Dirty Glory,* talks about going to visit the sites and, unexpectedly, some of the people involved in great spiritual revivals in the 1940's and 1950's on the Hebridean islands off the coast of Scotland, which began when two elderly sisters poured themselves out in prayer for their community. This seminal element of revival is not limited to "the old days." God is still calling Christians to love their neighbors, pray for them, and trust Him for the results. Robert Gribble tells very similar stories, but from a century earlier. May we see widespread revival in the 2040's as the Hebrides saw it in the 1940's and as Gribble saw it in the 1840's.

From the preface, "In this brief account of forty-two years' labour in the Gospel, [the author hopes] ...that many dear people of God will find some refreshment in the perusal of these pages, and he confidently hopes that they may also be used by the Lord for blessing to some who have hitherto been strangers to His grace and love. Should this happily be the case, his highest wishes will be gratified, and the glory shall be given to Him to whom alone it is due. The "Appendix" contains a few extracts from the writer's journal, added at the suggestion of friends, who considered that some account of the way in which the Lord has sustained him during the last twenty-five years, might form a suitable conclusion to the book...to show the providential care of an Heavenly

Father who delights to help those who trust in Him, and who, if able to raise such weak instruments in bringing sinners to Himself, can surely provide for His servant's daily need."

First published in 1858, this Christian classic has been refreshed by Walking Together Press so that perhaps, as this old book is presented to a new audience, it will encourage new readers to think like Gribble, asking the questions he did, "How can I be useful to the souls of others?" and "Lord, what wilt Thou have me to do?" The sweet stories in this book give us the encouragement that, should we ask such questions of God, He will certainly show us how to reach our own communities, even in our own post-Christian time.

Devotion 6: Impelled

THOUGH he had no formal training, Robert Gribble ended up spending more than forty years of his life as a highly effective minister of the Gospel, planting churches from village to village, in a pattern reminiscent of the Book of Acts. How this began is related in Gribble's own words.

When the Lord first made known His precious salvation to my own soul, the prevailing thought of my mind was, "how can I be useful to the souls of others?" I was continually inquiring, "Lord, what wilt Thou have me to do?" This desire if sincere and earnest, is never, I believe, disappointed; and it may be instructive to observe the way in which, in my case, the Lord was pleased to fulfil it... At that period, 1815, a village Sunday school was a new thing in that part of the country; ...the result... was the establishment of several within the space of one year, through my own personal exertions and the help of others who were stirred up to follow my example, so that nearly three hundred children were soon brought under religious instruction.

...The character of the whole agricultural population in that neighbourhood at this period was that of gross darkness. In a district nearly twenty miles in length there was scarcely any gospel ministry, nor did I know or hear of a single family—one only excepted—where the truth was known or valued....

A considerable crowd assembled within and around the cottage where the gospel was first preached in November 1815, and its results were interesting and important, far beyond any previous anticipation. A cry for the gospel was soon heard from these ignorant villagers, and it was responded to on some succeeding week evenings. This, however, did not satisfy, and I was earnestly intreated to provide a Sunday evening service also. But there was no one to undertake this. My heart yearned over the poor villagers, and I longed to send them the bread of life. At length I offered to read a sermon to them, and this was gladly accepted; and for a few weeks I read one of Burder's Village Sermons to a crowded congregation of rustic hearers. This was my first step in service for the Lord in the gospel. Up to this time I do not remember to have had a single thought of ministry, nor did I consider myself at all qualified for such a work, but I was now drawn into it as by necessity for the sake of others; and, as I then thought, merely to supply the present need. "But my thoughts are not your thoughts, saith the Lord;" and His word to me— although at that time I knew it not—was, "Arise and preach the preaching that I bid thee." Jonah 3:2

I was soon tired of reading a printed sermon and began to write one, and was gradually led from step to step until within less than twelve months I usually preached without notes.

I have stated thus much to show how one who, like myself, had received no preparatory instruction for ministry, was led to engage in a work so solemn and responsible; and that at a period, when both by Dissenters and Episcopalians, a certain measure of educational training either in some college or academy, was considered almost indispensable. I was fully aware of this, but was gradually led onwards, impelled by an agency I could not resist.

Theme

Holy Spirit directs believers in ministry
ACTS 8:29
The Spirit said to Philip, "Go near, and join yourself to this chariot."

Devotion

Robert Gribble's life of ministry began with two simple questions, "How can I be useful to the souls of others?" and "Lord, what wilt Thou have me to do?" He was sincere and earnest in asking these questions, willing to do anything in which the Lord would lead, including things he had never considered. "Up to this time I do not remember to have had a single thought of ministry, nor did I consider myself at all qualified for such a work..."

While Robert Gribble does not mention a clear voice like when the "Spirit said to Philip," God clearly led the Devonshire lay minister "by an agency [he] could not resist." It's also possible that Philip didn't actually hear a voice either. We simply know from the eighth chapter of Acts, and the story that unfolds with Philip talking to the Ethiopian, that he knew without a doubt that God was directing him. Probably, before meeting the Ethiopian, Philip had been asking God the same kinds of questions that Gribble asked. In other words, both Robert Gribble and Philip the Evangelist had made themselves unconditionally available for God's use, and both got to experience the thrilling adventures of partnering with God in his Kingdom.

For the past ten years, I have been asking similar questions, "Lord, what is it You are doing today?" and "How can I be a part of it?" Most often the answer to those questions is along the lines of, "Go do the dishes," because every "big" thing that God calls us to do is framed by a thousand tiny acts of obedience.

But also asking those questions led to the clear divine connection with the Jenta Reads team and all the opportunities that have arisen from it, including this book. Never would I have imagined that praying such questions would take me and my family to multiple African countries, places in Asia and Europe, nor result in such deep friendships, nor in such beautiful ministry to those in need.

Beware! Those are two very dangerous questions to ask if you are merely seeking to be comfortable. Asking those questions does not (necessarily) mean that God will send you to Africa. (In Robert Gribble's beautiful example, he never left Devonshire.) For me and my family, God has used our home as a place for needy people to stay, sometimes for a few years, while God ministered to them. He also sent us to Africa, because the question, "Lord, what are You doing today?" has no bounds! But the innumerable blessings, the thrilling adventures (Who knew dishes could be so exciting?), and the profound honor of partnering with God in what He is doing are worth more than any earthly comfort.

Reflection

Will you dare to ask the Father these two questions? "Lord, what is it You are doing today?" and "How can I be a part of it?" If you are sincere and earnest in asking those questions, be patient, stand back, and get ready to join God in the thrilling work of the expansion of His Kingdom!

❦

This story begins on page 1 of the Scripture Testimony Edition of *Recollections of an Evangelist* from Walking Together Press.

Devotion 7: Birthed in Prayer

A YOUNG man, simply identified as "S——," moved into Robert Gribble's neighborhood. They grew close and Gribble tells how the young man would "always [accompany] me in my journeys on the Lord's day, when our communion by the way was oftentimes very sweet." Upon taking new employment, the young man moved again to a different community. Being inspired by seeing God work powerfully during his times traveling with Gribble, he determined to seek God for something similar in this new neighborhood, and this is what happened:

> There were not any believing men at that time in the village, which lay close to the farm, except the farmer and one of his workmen, whose conversion is noticed in Chapter III; but as soon as S—— was settled in his cottage he determined to hold a prayer-meeting. He was told it would be of no use and no one would attend. S——, however, was not more conspicuous for love and zeal than for decision and firmness; and his immediate reply was, "then I will hold one by myself." The matter was of course settled, and it was immediately determined that his cottage should be used for a prayer-meeting at nine o'clock on Sunday mornings.

To the surprise of many this meeting was well attended from the beginning; and to the joy also of some it was often found to be a season of refreshment through the manifest tokens of the Lord's presence; proving that He is not confined to any building whatever, but may always be expected where but two or three meet in the name of Jesus. The blessing which this dear servant of God so earnestly desired to realise was not witheld. Some souls were born to God in his house, two of which I distinctly remember....

...The prayer-meeting was a means of much blessing in a place where vice and ungodliness were almost proverbial; and it was so well attended that a small chapel was considered needful. This object was so generally approved that it was completed without contracting any debt exactly one year after S——'s arrival in the village. The gospel preached within its walls has been used for bringing many souls to Christ. It was built to accommodate about one hundred hearers; but the attendance became so numerous that it was found needful to enlarge it about ten years after. I had quitted the neighbourhood some time previous, but was present at its reopening, when my heart was made glad by witnessing the blessed effects of the gospel. The whole character of the village was changed; many stubborn hearts had yielded to the influence of truth, and the number of believers appeared to be larger in proportion to the whole population than in any other village with which I was acquainted.

Theme

All great movements of God are birthed in prayer
ACTS 1:14

> Then they returned to Jerusalem from the mountain called Olivet, which is near Jerusalem, a Sabbath day's journey away. When they had come in, they went up into the upper room where they were staying; that is Peter, John, James, Andrew, Philip, Thomas, Bartholomew, Matthew, James the son of Alphaeus, Simon the

Zealot, and Judas the son of James. *All these with one accord continued steadfastly in prayer and supplication,* along with the women, and Mary the mother of Jesus, and with his brothers. (Acts 1:12-14 emphasis added)

Devotion

D. L. Moody is attributed to the saying, "Every great movement of God can be traced to a kneeling figure."

The disciples were gathered together in prayer for many days, not knowing what was next, but continuing in faith that He wanted them to pray (Acts 1). Then perhaps the greatest, and certainly the most famous, movement of God came about after this time of corporate prayer. (Acts 2)

If there is one constant theme in the books of the *Scripture Testimony Collection,* it is that God answers prayer, and every answered prayer certainly represents a move of the living and loving God, whether large or small. Robert Gribble's friend, S——, believed this about God. He was willing—alone if necessary—to simply pray and wait upon God for whatever He had in store for the community.

Reflection

Heavenly Father, gives us Your heart for those around us. Lead us into prayer. Delight our souls with the anticipation of Your powerful action. Grant us the patience to persist while we wait for your perfect time.

※

This story begins on page 25 of the Scripture Testimony Edition of *Recollections of an Evangelist* from Walking Together Press.

Chapter V

Hudson Taylor: The Man who believed God

I N missionary circles, Hudson Taylor, founder of the China Inland Mission, is a household name. Probably he is the most influential missionary in post-Biblical times. At the time of this writing, in the early twenty-first century, there may be as many as two hundred million believers in the Chinese underground church. These are Christians who are willing to suffer potential societal consequences for their "illegal" faith in Christ, from lost opportunities to outright physical persecution, which means they are serious about following Jesus. It is safe to say that a vast number, if not the majority, of these believers can trace their faith lineage back to Jesus through Hudson Taylor. It's not that he was such an effective evangelist, he certainly was, but more that he inspired, supported, and otherwise walked alongside thousands of missionaries both inside and outside the China Inland Mission.

Almost immediately after coming to faith as a teenager, Hudson Taylor felt the call of God to China. He felt an ever-increasing burden for the millions in China who had never heard the glad tidings of the Gospel. While he had no idea how he was going to get there, he knew that he could trust God with the details, as well as whatever provision would be required. Taylor sought practical training that would naturally bring him into intimate contact with Chinese people, so he studied in London to be a medical doctor. Equally important, during the years of medical school he was also enrolled in the "school of faith," determined to only ever ask his Heavenly Father to supply his needs. This meant often going without until the very last moment, when God would provide in such a way as to make it clear that He was the source.

In 1865 Hudson Taylor visited George Müller and his orphanage in Bristol, England. Taylor was determined to run the nascent China Inland Mission (CIM) on the same principles of faith as exemplified by George Müller, who promised to pray, which *meant* something. Then for the next twenty years Müller also provided financial support and encouragement. In 1886, the aged George Müller was able to visit Hudson Taylor and many of the CIM missionaries in China.

Hudson Taylor was certainly endowed with great leadership qualities and people skills, but it was his faith in God that inspired so many others. We can see this influence among the people represented in the *Scripture Testimony Collection.* Jonathan and Rosalind Goforth, Amy Carmichael, and Sadhu Sundar Singh were often inspired by Taylor to trust God for their needs. In some cases Taylor prayed for, and wrote letters of encouragement to these people, even though none was affiliated with the CIM.

In 2005, my wife and I, along with our five (and then six) children worked as full time missionaries on the Mexican border. Inspired by reading Hudson Taylor's story, we went by faith, only ever asking God to supply our needs. In the time we were there, we never went hungry, never lacked for our children, and never missed a payment. Nearly always from a different source, God provided everything in answer to prayer. I can't say that it was always easy, God allowed us to be tested, and there is a good reason why Jesus says, "Don't be anxious," because it's natural. Hudson Taylor was wonderfully transparent about these things too.

He trusted only God for all temporal supplies for himself, his family, and more than eight hundred missionaries that joined him in more than fifty years of Gospel labor. While these are impressive numbers, Hudson Taylor was first and foremost a child of God, constantly growing in his faith. One of Taylor's greatest gifts to posterity is the transparency with which he wrote about life challenges and his own faith journey. Marshall Broomhall, a cousin of Hudson Taylor and editorial secretary of the China Inland Mission, wrote *Hudson Taylor, The Man who believed God,* in order to both provide a shorter biography (the previous one by Taylor's son was over 1200 pages), and to focus more on the character of Hudson Taylor instead of the larger story of the China Inland Mission.

From the author's foreword, "There can be no doubt but that Hudson Taylor's acts have helped to mould men's minds, and have given an impulse to missionary activity and methods.... And there can be no question as to the great idea with which he was possessed, and to which he attached himself. His life was dominated from first to last by his conviction as to the utter faithfulness of God. It is for this reason that the title of this little book has been called: *Hudson Taylor: The Man who believed God.*"

Originally published in 1929, Walking Together Press has refreshed this Christian classic in order to present the encouragement of Hudson Taylor's faith in God to a new audience. Truly, you *must read* this book. In the meantime, here are a few devotional lessons from Hudson Taylor's life.

Devotion 8: The Burning Hot Coin

HUDSON Taylor spent years in preparation for his life-calling of being a missionary in China. Even more important than learning the practical skills of medicine, he had entered into the school of faith.

"When I get out to China," he said to himself, "I shall have no claim on anyone for anything. My only claim will be on God. How important to learn before leaving England, to move man through God by prayer alone...."

Two lessons in this school of faith were now learned which were a help to him for the rest of his life, and to these reference must be made. Though his employer had requested him to remind him when his salary was due, he determined not to do this, that he might thus test his faith. On one occasion his quarterly salary was due but no allusion had been made to it, and he found himself with only two shillings and sixpence in his pocket. At this juncture he was asked by a poor man to go and pray with his wife who was dying. He went and found a squalid room in which were four or five half-starved children, and their mother, lying on a wretched pallet, with a three-day-old babe crying at her breast. The clamant need of this poor woman, and his own limited circumstances, led to a spiritual conflict such as he said he had never experienced before, and possibly never since. He tried to pray but could not. He felt it would be mocking God to ask His aid while he withheld his own half-crown, and yet—that was all he had! Had it been two shillings and a sixpence he could have given part, but it was a half-crown piece, so his gift must be all or nothing. In vain he tried to speak words of comfort, until he felt a hypocrite himself, since he could not trust God with an empty pocket. Filled with distress he rose at length from his knees, only to have the distracted father say to him, "If you can help us, for God's sake do." At that moment the Lord's words, "Give to him that asketh of thee," flashed through his mind, and, as he said afterwards, "In the word of a King there is power." Thrusting his hand into his pocket he drew out his last and only coin, and gave it to the man. The struggle had been keen and crucial, but joy now flooded his soul.

"Not only was the poor woman's life saved," he subsequently wrote, "but my life, as I fully realised, had been saved too. It might have been a wreck—probably would have been as a Christian life—had not grace at that time conquered and the striving of God's Spirit been obeyed."

Home he went that night with a heart as light as his pocket, but with the dark, deserted streets resounding with his praise. Before retiring to rest he asked the Lord that the loan might be a short one, for otherwise he would have no dinner next day. The morning came and with it the postman, who delivered a letter containing half a sovereign and a pair of gloves! "Four hundred per cent for twelve hours' investment!" he exclaimed, and there and then determined that God's bank, that could not break, should henceforth have his savings or his earnings, as the case might be.

Theme

Give to everyone who asks

MATTHEW 5:42

Give to him who asks you, and don't turn away him who desires to borrow from you.

ACTS 20:35

In all things I gave you an example, that so laboring you ought to help the weak, and to remember the words of the Lord Jesus, that he himself said, 'It is more blessed to give than to receive.'"

I JOHN 3:17

But whoever has the world's goods and sees his brother in need, then closes his heart of compassion against him, how does God's love remain in him?

God using an inner voice to communicate

ACTS 11:12

The *Spirit told me* to go with them, without discriminating. These six brothers also accompanied me, and we entered into the man's house. (emphasis added)

JOHN 14:26

But the Counselor, the Holy Spirit, whom the Father will send in my name, will teach you all things, and *will remind you of all that I said to you.* (emphasis added)

Devotion

Sometimes the will of God is obvious, and the choice to obey or disobey becomes a watershed moment in the life of faith. On that fateful day Hudson Taylor's character of simple trust in God was tested and proved. Taylor had no idea how this simple obedience would go on to affect the eternal destinies of literally millions of people.

"...he felt a hypocrite himself, since he could not trust God with an empty pocket," but, "In the word of a King there is power."

In the midst of the situation, Hudson Taylor's conscience bothered him. He couldn't pray freely, nor could he give genuine encouragement to the poor suffering family. He was miserable. But it wasn't until the Holy Spirit "brought to remembrance" (John 14:26) the words of

Jesus, the King, that the clear choice was before him. It was as if God was saying, "Well Hudson, my son, will you obey Me or not?" This was truly a defining moment. To disobey such a clear voice from the Holy Spirit would have brought Him grief.

Reflection

Is God calling you to a particularly difficult act of obedience? Or perhaps He is only reminding you of a regular, small act of obedience. In either case, each act of obedience to the will of God is a watershed moment, leading us to be more like Christ...or not.

C. S. Lewis in his book, *Mere Christianity,* presents an example of a man growing better through tiny acts of obedience. *Today he has not kicked the cat.*

※

This story begins on page 34 of the Scripture Testimony Edition of *Hudson Taylor, the Man who believed God* from Walking Together Press.

Devotion 9: Trials, Deliverance, and Powerful Witness

As a young medical student in London, Hudson Taylor had concurrent enrollment in the much more important, and often times more difficult School of Faith, where he learned great lessons of trust, and in hearing the voice of God.

Still faith did not always come easily, and his dogged determination was at times severely taxed.

"Though the heavens have seemed as brass," he wrote, "and I have felt myself left and forsaken, I have been enabled to cling to the promises by simple naked faith, as father calls it."

Such words as these were not lightly written, as one or two episodes in his life in London prove.

The husband of his former landlady in Hull was Chief Officer in a ship which sailed from London, and Hudson Taylor, ever willing to assist, offered to receive this man's monthly half-pay and remit the same to Hull to save the woman a commission. On one occasion, as he was working for a scholarship, and could not very well spare time to call at the office, he advanced the money out of his own pocket. But when he did call he was informed, much to his consternation, that as the officer had deserted, and gone off to the gold diggings, his pay had been stopped. Hudson Taylor knew it was useless to ask the woman in Hull to refund what he had advanced, and, somewhat philosophically, recognized that, at the most, it meant that the day when he would have been cast upon God for fresh supplies was only being forestalled.

But this was not all, for soon after this he poisoned his finger when dissecting the body of a person who had died from a malignant fever. Sudden and severe sickness ensued, and the demonstrator, a skilful surgeon at the hospital, urged him to drive home in a hansom at full speed, for, said he, "you are a dead man."

But to take a hansom was not possible without the means to pay; yet even then the thought which most distressed him was, "Is China an empty dream after all?" But an assurance that he would live, and not die before his work was done, took possession of him, and though exceedingly ill he set out to walk the four miles home. But his strength failed him, and only after much suffering did he succeed in reaching his room by the aid of a bus.

The weeks which followed were full of pain, and for a time his life literally hung in the balance. At length, however, after a prolonged period of acute prostration, he was able to leave his room. Now he was urged by the doctor to go home, into the country, for much-needed refreshment. But he had no money for his fare, and he had withheld even the news of his illness from his parents. What then was he to do?

At this juncture it was deeply impressed upon him that he should call again at the Shipping Offices and make fresh inquiries. This seemed a hopeless undertaking. The office was two miles away; he had no money even for a bus, and he was so weak he had even to seek assistance in going downstairs. After all, what was the use of going? Was not this an empty impulse, he asked himself, the mere clutching at a straw, or some mental process of his own, as a last resort, and not God's guidance? But no, he felt the impulse was God-given, and so he set out, to quote his own words, "Not to attempt to walk, but to walk to Cheapside."

...It was a long two miles to the city... and when at length he did reach his destination he was obliged to rest outside on the doorstep, despite the curious gaze of City men, ere he mounted the stairs to the office. But faith and endurance were rewarded. The money previously withheld, and more since due, was actually waiting for him, for it had been discovered that the man who had deserted was not the officer in question, but an able-bodied seaman of the same name. And thus he obtained not only what was sufficient for his journey home, but the balance for remitting to the officer's wife in Hull.

The mere recital of these experiences to the doctor who had attended him, who was a sceptic, called forth the following remark, uttered with tears in his eyes, "I would give all the world for a faith like yours." And who can say how timely that testimony was, for these two never met again. A sudden stroke, followed by a brief period of helpless waiting in the country, and the doctor's last call came. "I cannot but entertain the hope," wrote Hudson Taylor, "that the Master was speaking to him through His dealings with me, and that I shall meet him in the Better Land."

Theme

Signs and wonders draw attention to the Gospel message
JOHN 4:28-29

So the woman left her water pot, went away into the city, and said to the people, "Come, see a man who told me everything that I did. Can this be the Christ?"

ACTS 8:5-8

The multitudes listened with one accord to the things that were spoken by Philip when they heard and saw the signs which he did. (Acts 8:6)

God using an inner voice to communicate
ACTS 10:19-20
> While Peter was pondering the vision, *the Spirit said to him,* "Behold, three men seek you. But arise, get down, and go with them, doubting nothing; for I have sent them." (emphasis added)

God's work will not lack God's supply
PHILIPPIANS 4:19
> My God will supply every need of yours according to his riches in glory in Christ Jesus.

Devotion

The lessons of this story are not about the details of Hudson Taylor's experiences, which are unique to him. But there are several important things to take away for any follower of Jesus.

While this particular series of events may seem extreme, we should not be surprised that difficulties in life often heap up together. The Apostle Peter reminds us to "...not be surprised at the fiery ordeal that has come on you to test you, as though something strange were happening to you." (1 Peter 4:12) Because of our fallen and broken world, these kinds of things inevitably happen to anyone. Jesus said, "In this world *you will have* trouble. But take heart! I have overcome the world." (John 16:33 emphasis added)

As Peter said, every trial is a test. What will we do with it? How will we respond? Will we take the natural human route of petulant complaint and despair? Or will we take heart, and seek the Lord for the *super*-natural response to overcome? Hudson Taylor sought the Lord in the midst of the trials, knowing that His calling was sure (i.e. that the sickness would not be fatal), and knowing that He had promised to provide. In this posture, Taylor was able to hear God's inner voice, even with all the noise of suffering and lack.

But the greatest lesson is how God uses miraculous signs and wonders to get the attention of unbelievers. You may be thinking that this is an overstatement of this story. Of course Hudson Taylor recovered from a fatal illness, and of course God supplied his material needs, but are these really miraculous signs and wonders? The fact is... The way he responded in faith to all these difficulties is simply not natural human behavior. It is profoundly supernatural. It is the fruit of faith in God the Father, and it brought the skeptical physician to tears.

Reflection

Romans 14:7 says, "For none of us lives for ourselves alone, and none of us dies for ourselves alone." Whether we think so or not, our lives affect those around us profoundly. As Jesus said, the light of our lives is shining before others.

Perhaps people skeptical of Christianity are not as concerned with stories of miraculous healing, as they are with how a Jesus follower handles the everyday difficulties of life, and those common human temptations to complain or blame. When Jesus in us overcomes the natural tendencies of the world, people notice.

Will we sink to the natural human level of response when trials come our way? Or will we seek God, in faith, in the midst of the trials? By doing so, not only will we find Him and His deliverance, but the resulting story will be powerful in the lives of others.

This story begins on page 43 of the Scripture Testimony Edition of *Hudson Taylor, the Man who believed God* from Walking Together Press.

Devotion 10: Becoming All Things to All Men

HUDSON Taylor was not the first Western missionary to adopt Chinese dress and customs. Yet he was convinced that it was the right thing to do, in imitation of his precious Lord Jesus who became like one of us. In the following passage from *Hudson Taylor, The Man who believed God,* Marshall Broomhall gives us Hudson Taylor's powerful argument in his own words.

"Had our Lord appeared on earth as an angel of light, He would doubtless have inspired far more awe and reverence, and would have collected together even larger multitudes to attend His ministry. But to save man He became man, not merely like man, but very man.... In language, in costume, in everything unsinful, He made Himself one with those He sought to benefit.

"Had He been born a noble Roman, rather than a Jew, He would, perhaps, if less loved, have commanded more of a certain kind of respect; and He would assuredly thereby have been spared much indignity to which He was subjected. This, however, was not His aim; He emptied Himself. Surely no follower of the meek and lowly Jesus will be likely to conclude that it is 'beneath the dignity of a Christian missionary' to seek identification with this poor people, in the hope that he may see them washed, sanctified, and justified in the name of the Lord Jesus, and by the Spirit of our God!...

"I am not peculiar in holding the opinion that the foreign dress and carriage of missionaries—to a certain extent affected by some of their converts and pupils—the foreign appearance of the chapels, and, indeed, the foreign air given to everything connected with religion, have very largely hindered the rapid dissemination of the truth among the Chinese. But why should such a foreign aspect be given to Christianity? The Word of God does not require it; nor, I conceive, could sound reason justify it."

"Let us in everything not sinful, become Chinese, that by all means we may save some. Let us adopt their costume, acquire their language, study to imitate their habits, and approximate to their diet as far as health and constitution will allow. Let us live in their houses, making no unnecessary alterations in external form, and only as far modifying their internal arrangements as attention to health and efficiency for work absolutely require....

"This cannot, of course, be attained without some measure of inconvenience.... But will anyone reflect on what He gave up who left heaven's throne to be cradled in a manger... who being the Loved One of the Father, never unappreciated, never misunderstood, and receiving the ceaseless adoration of the hierarchies of heaven, became a despised Nazarene, misunderstood by His most faithful followers, suspected by those who owed to Him their very being, and whose salvation He had come to seek; and finally, mocked, and spit upon, crucified and slain, with thieves, bandits, and outlaws. Will, I ask, any brother or sister reflect on this, and yet hesitate to make the trifling sacrifice to which we have alluded?...

"But, once let the question arise, 'Are we called to give up this, or that, or the other?' or admit the thought, 'I did not expect this or that privation or inconvenience,' and your service will cease to be that free and happy one which is most conducive to efficiency and success. 'God loveth a cheerful giver.'"

There is much more in the same spirit, but this must suffice to show how truly he had apprehended the mind of his Master, and to indicate the spirit he sought to infuse in those who wished to follow him. That he was not asking what he did not practise himself all knew, and that added power to his words.

Theme

Become all things to all people
I CORINTHIANS 9:19-23

> For though I was free from all, I brought myself under bondage to all, that I might gain the more. To the Jews I became as a Jew, that I might gain Jews; to those who are under the law, as under the law, that I might gain those who are under the law; to those who are without law, as without law (not being without law toward God, but under law toward Christ), that I might win those who are without law. To the weak I became as weak, that I might gain the weak. I have become all things to all men, that I may by all means save some. Now I do this for the sake of the Good News, that I may be a joint partaker of it.

Devotion

There is an unfortunate parallel between the position of the nineteenth-century Westerner in China and that of a Roman citizen in first-century Palestine. The various Western governments had bullied the Chinese for the sake of trade and territorial control. And even more insidious than overt military might, the West had introduced opium to China, benefiting from it like any common despicable drug dealer of our time. To be a Westerner, and to live in the secure islands of Western culture in the various Chinese cities, was to project fear and intimidation on the average Chinese citizen, much like the first-century Romans did over the occupied Jews. All this lends tremendous weight to Hudson Taylor's argument that an ambassador of Christ should divest himself of any perceived advantage and like the Apostle Paul said, become as a Chinese person, that they might gain some.

More than that, to identify with people, and to respect them so much as to become like them, to speak their language, to eat their food, to dwell as they do, is to love them like yourself... because you have made yourself like them. This is precisely what our loving God did for us in the incarnation.

And Paul is not merely talking about an effective missionary method. He takes it to another level when he says, "Now I do this for the sake of the Good News, *that I may be a joint partaker of it."* What is the Good News? It is that the Kingdom of God is here, because the King is here. What is the Kingdom like? It is a community. It is a family. Paul is not merely talking about "gaining" converts, like so many notches in his belt, or so many statistics to report back to the mission supporters, but he is gaining brothers and sisters—peers—with whom he shares the blessings of the Good News, which is to be in God's family together.

Reflection

Heavenly Father, help us to see those who don't yet know You, as our potential brothers and sisters; peers in your Kingdom. Help us to identify with them, that we might win their friendship, and win their hearts for you.

ॐ

This story begins on page 115 of the Scripture Testimony Edition of *Hudson Taylor, The Man who believed God* from Walking Together Press.

Chapter VI

Answered or Unanswered, Miracles of Faith in China

L ouisa Vaughan was an American Presbyterian missionary in China who lived in the present reality of God, and wrote a beautiful and engaging collection of stories testifying to that reality. Two subjects of faith recur in almost every story; that the believer can ask anything in the name of Jesus based on His promise in John 14:13-14, and that via prayer and repentance, genuine revival comes through a visitation of the Holy Spirit.

Written at a time of rising cultural skepticism regarding prayer, Louisa Vaughan wrote of her first-hand experiences and eye-witness testimony of the loving, prayer-answering God. Is it unscientific to believe that we can pray for anything, from day to day needs, to a person's conversion, to the end of a drought? "Answered -or- Unanswered?" is the challenge posed to the reader by the eighteen stories of prayer in this little book.

From the author's preface, "The aim of this little volume is to set forth as simply, and as concisely as possible, the incidents connected with my life and service for the Lord Jesus during my residence in

China from October, 1896, to January, 1912. These stories as written were the result of the vision which the Lord Himself gave me concerning my witness-bearing amongst the Chinese people. And this testimony was to be one of Faith..."

Originally published in 1920, this Christian classic has been refreshed in order to be presented to a new audience. Since Jesus is the same yesterday, today, and forever, these stories of God's faithfulness are as relevant and inspiring today as they were a century ago, because God still answers prayer. Following are two devotional lessons from this delightful book.

Devotion 11: Jesus Makes People Good

As a single-woman missionary in rural China, Louisa Vaughan relied on hired help so that she could spend her time teaching and preaching. More than once God used these circumstances to bring the light of the Gospel in unexpected ways, showing that being a missionary is not a specific set of religious tasks, but rather the way of the Christian life. The following story illustrates this point.

> For the second time in my life in China I was considering the problem of getting a cook....
>
> In my helplessness I betook myself to prayer. My petition was that my Lord would send me the man He desired me to have. It is likely if I had prayed, "Please, dear Lord, send me just such another man as I have had, efficient, reliable, honest, and a Christian," I might have had my prayer answered exactly as I requested. If it had occurred to me to remember that my Father in Heaven had sent His Son to die for the lost, I might have saved myself quite a little anxiety, but I did not. I needed a cook, so I prayed for one. Days passed. The only candidate for the position was my neighbor's boy, a young man with an awful reputation. Of course, a missionary could not possibly employ a man of that kind. Mr. Hwoa, the

Chinese teacher, turned him down once, twice, three times. During all these days I wondered why my prayer was not answered.

One day I stepped into my study and waiting for me was a brisk-looking young Chinese man. He soon told me his business—a cook desiring to work for me. Lived next door! To my horror it was the same individual back again. Resolutely determined to put a stop to his hopes once and forever, I inquired if he knew the reputation he bore, reciting for his benefit the list of sins I had heard he was guilty of—lying, drinking, stealing, gambling, etc.

He patiently listened until I finished, and then in a gentle voice said, "Well, didn't you come to my country to teach us to be good?" Completely non-plussed, I could find no words to reply. After a lengthy pause, I said: "I was not aware you wanted to learn to be good."

"Oh, yes, that is exactly what I want," he said, "someone to teach me to be good. I heard you taught the Chinese women, so I came to you to learn."

Still fearful of some hidden desire to work evil upon me, I discouraged him in every way. "Have you ever tried to be good? It is not so easy as you seem to imagine," I suggested, and other remarks of a like nature, but nothing discouraged him. I realized there was no escape. He was determined to learn to be good and from me! Well, I thought, I shall put the bars up so high he cannot hold out, and in that way I shall be through with him in a few days.

Addressing him aloud, I said: "Well, I shall give you one chance. Now, understand, just one chance. If I find you once, only once, drinking, gambling, lying, or going to the market without my permission, then you must leave my house, never to return. Many times since I have thought of myself in connection with this boy of eighteen. Suppose the Lord had given me only one chance, I, who had failed again and again. Wang Si Fu—that was his name— agreed to my conditions....

On his arrival on the next day I immediately began to pray for his conversion, which occurred in less than a week. We were at morning prayers. I had taught him in the meantime to pray, "Heavenly Father, forgive me my sins. Cleanse me from them in the precious blood of Jesus. Fill me with Thy Holy Spirit. In Jesus' Name." God abundantly answered that prayer, beyond all I could ask or think.

The cook's tragic personal story is worth reading in full, but suffice it to say that he encountered various injustices to which he responded by running away. In time he fell into bad company, and into a life of vice and evil that brought shame to his family.

When I heard his tale I sent him home to beg his parents' forgiveness for his lack of filial duty. The village was distant four miles from Tsing Tau. About two hundred people lived there and they were all sur-named "Wang." Every person in the village was a relative, far off or near, of my cook.

His announcement to his family and village was: "I have learned to be good and have returned to give you an opportunity to see for yourselves a changed man." Wonder, consternation and quite a percentage of criticism prevailed when he declared that being good involved leaving the spirits of his ancestors to their own devices, giving them neither worship nor offerings, turning away from idols and accepting God's Son, Jesus Christ, as his Saviour. This Saviour, being God's Son, was able to save him in this world from sin and Satan, and afterwards give him a mansion in Heaven. There was nothing to say. Every mouth was closed, every tongue was dumb. He was good. No more gambling, no more drinking, and his wages saved and brought home to his mother, a positive proof that he was a changed man. Wang Si Fu was a new creature in Christ Jesus.

After his second visit there could be no further doubt. He was a good man, a new creation forth from the hand of God, a miracle of love and grace. All could see. Blessed simplicity of God's plan....

Theme

Salvation transforms
2 CORINTHIANS 5:17

> Therefore if anyone is in Christ, he is a new creation. The old things have passed away. Behold, all things have become new.

True disciples forsake the old self and put on the new self
EPHESIANS 4:20-5:20

> This I say therefore, and testify in the Lord, that you no longer walk as the rest of the Gentiles also walk, in the futility of their mind, being darkened in their understanding, alienated from the life of God because of the ignorance that is in them, because of the hardening of their hearts. They, having become callous, gave themselves up to lust, to work all uncleanness with greediness. But you didn't learn Christ that way, if indeed you heard him, and were taught in him, even as truth is in Jesus: *that you put away, as concerning your former way of life,* the old man that grows corrupt after the lusts of deceit, and that you be renewed in the spirit of your mind, and *put on the new man,* who in the likeness of God has been created in righteousness and holiness of truth. (Ephesians 4:17-24 emphasis added)

COLOSSIANS 3:5-17

> *Put to death* therefore your members which are on the earth: sexual immorality, uncleanness, depraved passion, evil desire, and covetousness, which is idolatry... *put them all away:* anger, wrath, malice, slander, and shameful speaking out of your mouth. Don't lie to one another, seeing that you have *put off the old man* with his doings, and have *put on the new man,* who is being renewed in knowledge after the image of his Creator... (from Colossians 3:5-10 emphasis added)

Devotion

It is not sufficient to simply learn the right things to do, or as the young man put it, "to learn to be good." One can know what is good and right, but lack the power—the motivation—to do it. In fact, Wang Si Fu already knew the right things to do, or rather, not to do. He already knew that his vices were evil, and that he was powerless to overcome them. But God honored his humble beginning; a desire to be good, somehow...

Louisa Vaughan taught him the one thing—the only thing—to do in order to be good, which is to surrender to God. *"Heavenly Father, forgive me my sins. Cleanse me from them in the precious blood of Jesus. Fill me with Thy Holy Spirit. In Jesus' Name."*

When a person surrenders to Christ, he or she becomes a new person. Jesus describes this as being born again. This person gets a completely new beginning, with completely different, *spiritual* DNA. (John 3:3) The Apostle Paul describes this process as becoming a *new creature,* in which all the things of the old creature have passed away, giving way to new things. (2 Corinthians 5:17) As profound as these truths are to this new, born-again creature; to the people observing, they are merely words.

Through the indwelling power of the Holy Spirit, Wang Si Fu had put off his old behaviors, and had put on new ones. He came home and said, "I have learned to be good and have returned to give you an opportunity to see for yourselves a changed man." Then in bringing money home to support his mother, in standing fast in his faith against the idol worship that had been normal to him since childhood, and in forsaking old vices, the proof of the words was plain for all to see.

Reflection

Have you been born again? Have you surrendered to Christ? Have you asked Him to be Master of your life? If so, then He promises the indwelling power of His Holy Spirit to help you take off the smelly old clothes of the flesh-oriented life, and to put on the fresh new clothes of the Kingdom of God.

✻

This story begins on page 83 of the Scripture Testimony Edition of *Answered or Unanswered?* from Walking Together Press.

Devotion 12: Please Come Help Us

IN the last devotion we learned the story of Wang Si Fu and his miraculous rebirth into a man who had "learned to be good." The story continues as his beautiful transformation became contagious. Picking up the story again...

> His announcement to his family and village was: "I have learned to be good and have returned to give you an opportunity to see for yourselves a changed man." Wonder, consternation and quite a percentage of criticism prevailed when he declared that being good involved leaving the spirits of his ancestors to their own devices, giving them neither worship nor offerings, turning away from idols and accepting God's Son, Jesus Christ, as his Saviour. This Saviour, being God's Son, was able to save him in this world from sin and Satan, and afterwards give him a mansion in Heaven. There was nothing to say. Every mouth was closed, every tongue was dumb. He was good. No more gambling, no more drinking, and his wages saved and brought home to his mother, a positive proof that he was a changed man. Wang Si Fu was a new creature in Christ Jesus.
> After his second visit there could be no further doubt. He was a good man, a new creation forth from the hand of God, a miracle

of love and grace. All could see. Blessed simplicity of God's plan. Would that it were used more in this country.

In a few weeks I received a long letter written in Chinese, signed by the village elders, three of them over ninety years of age, Wang's great-grandfather and two great-granduncles. Would I be kind enough, they wrote, to visit their village and preach this new doctrine, which could make men good. I wrote in reply, telling them it was neither Chinese nor Western etiquette for a woman teacher to preach, but I would send the evangelist in a few days to teach them. In less than a week Mr. Hwoa, the native evangelist, visited their village. They entertained him in a kindly, liberal fashion, but never once invited him to preach. Returning, he informed me that they were nothing but a lot of hypocrites; they had no intention of learning the doctrine, or becoming Christians; they did not wish to listen. I thought it very strange, but said nothing, accepting his report without question. A few weeks later another letter arrived with the same request: "Would I be gracious enough to visit their unworthy village and teach them this new doctrine?" I again refused, but suggested Mr. S., a fellow missionary, as an excellent substitute. A third letter came, saying very plainly, "We have no doubt Mr. S. is all you say, but up till this time we have not had opportunity to see his work. We have seen yours, so please come over and help us. We desire to learn from you. Oh, come and teach us. We are hungry to learn." These people were heathen, so did not understand it was the Lord's work they had seen.

Needless to say, I finally went, taking Wang Si Fu along. Three Chinese women who loved the Lord accompanied us. Four days were spent going to and from this village. Today there is a large group of Christians here who gather for worship in Wang's home.

My adopted son, as Wang liked to call himself, would not cook for any other missionary. After he found out I was not returning to China he wrote me to say he had gone home and was in some small business, where he had freedom to preach Jesus, whom he loved.

Theme

Unbelievers pleading to hear the Gospel
ACTS 16:9-10

A vision appeared to Paul in the night. There was a man of Macedonia standing, begging him, and saying, "Come over into Macedonia and help us." When he had seen the vision, immediately we sought to go out to Macedonia, concluding that the Lord had called us to preach the Good News to them.

Devotion

"Please come over and help us...Oh, come teach us. We are hungry to learn." While Miss Vaughan did not receive a vision like the Apostle Paul, she did receive persistent letters with language that truly paralleled his famous missionary call to Macedonia.

There are no details given in the Book of Acts about the situation in Macedonia, but it's not hard to imagine a similar scenario. Perhaps a formerly profligate son of a Macedonian village had been over the Aegean Sea to some place where the Gospel had taken hold, and had returned good. His change was so obvious to everyone that they simply had to know of this new doctrine. Perhaps in their desperation to know how to get this goodness inside of themselves, and with some basic direction from their renewed son, they dared to pray to God for help. And the rest is history.

Why was Louisa Vaughan so reluctant to go preach to the people at their request? Perhaps she was concerned that they thought she had some special talent or power or program that could make men good, for she says, "These people were heathen, so did not understand it was the Lord's work they had seen."

Ultimately she went, and was able to explain that the Gospel is not a self-improvement program in which one can learn to be good. Rather it is the Good News that, through surrendering to Jesus Christ, we can be made right with God. And then He works in us to make us good.

Reflection

Augustine of Hippo said, "For that good thing which makes men good is God."*

☒☒

This story begins on page 86 of the Scripture Testimony Edition of *Answered or Unanswered?* from Walking Together Press.

---

* Thomas, Aquinas. 1874. *Catena aurea, commentary on the four Gospels; collected out of the works of the Fathers.* Oxford, Parker. p. 275

Chapter VII

Goforth of China

A LMOST from the moment of his conversion at eighteen years of age, Jonathan Goforth was an evangelist. In addition to tireless itinerant preaching, constant evangelism in slums, and even brothels, one summer during his years at Knox College, he visited nine hundred sixty Toronto families. It was said of Jonathan Goforth that, "When he found his own soul needed Jesus Christ, it became a passion with him to take Jesus Christ to every soul." This passion led him to devote his life to the cause of spreading the Gospel in China, and also caught the attention of twenty-year-old artist, Rosalind Bell-Smith.

Goforth of China is the biography of Jonathan Goforth, written *by his wife.* Therefore it is also the beautiful story of their marriage and family, and a lifetime of team ministry. Rosalind was somewhat spunky herself. She tells of how the first time she saw Jonathan was at a Saturday meeting she almost didn't attend, until her brother told her she couldn't. "I was on the point of saying this was impossible, when my brother whispered, 'You have no time. You are going to England.' Partly to show him I could do as I pleased—what a trifle

75

can turn the course of a life—I said to Mr. O'Brien, 'Very well; expect me on Saturday.'"

She had seen Jonathan Goforth briefly before that Saturday meeting, and was struck with his eyes. When he went forward to speak at the meeting, he turned and set his Bible on his chair. Rosalind, suddenly impulsive, got up and reached across several people to pick up the Bible. She then returned to her seat and surreptitiously rifled through its well-worn and heavily marked pages. She then returned the Bible to the chair and said to herself, "This is the man I would like to marry!"

Jonathan and Rosalind Goforth were Presbyterian missionaries in China from 1888 to 1935. They were pioneers in many ways, including "family ministry," where they included their children in their travels and evangelistic work. While they did not work under the China Inland Mission, they were personally encouraged and counseled by Hudson Taylor, who had been influential in the Goforth's commitment to China as missionaries. At the same time, the China Inland Mission was indebted to Jonathan Goforth, whose address at the same conference where Rosalind pilfered his Bible, stirred the heart of Dr. Henry W. Frost to be a missionary. Dr. Frost went on to become the North American Director of the China Inland Mission.

The family endured harrowing trials and narrowly escaped death during the 1900 Boxer Rebellion. Then in the early 1900's, Dr. Goforth sought the "greater works than these" that Jesus promises in John 14:12. Goforth became a student of revivals, both contemporary and historical, and for the rest of his missionary career he worked as a revivalist, witnessing the powerful work of the Holy Spirit in the lives of thousands.

Rosalind Goforth became a prolific author of books on missions and answered prayer. In this biography she provides tender and unvarnished glimpses into the life of her beloved husband, who was just as godly a man in private as he was in public. From the introduction, "Dr. and Mrs. Goforth were given of God to each other. It was a marriage of rare beauty, fellowship, and unity in faith and work. They were a rich blessing to all who entered their home in China, in Manchuria, or in Canada, and they brought a rich blessing into every home they entered. When Mrs. Goforth's hearing was impaired, Dr. Goforth was ears for her; and she, in his blindness, was eyes for him. But no physical weaknesses or limitations ever stopped their enthusiastic labors in winning souls for their Lord. May He bless this life-story to the raising up of many to walk in their footsteps, till the Lord come."

Goforth of China is truly a *must-read* Christian classic. It is delightfully and intimately written, giving a glimpse into a couple that exudes the warm love of Jesus. Following are two devotionals to further introduce the book.

Devotion 13: Open House, Open Hearts

Jonathan and Rosalind Goforth were like the faithful servants to whom the Master entrusted the talents. (Matthew 25:14-30) While they had a home in which they had many household items, they saw these as resources to be spent (sometimes literally) on behalf of others, which is powerfully illustrated by the following:

> Early in 1896, Presbytery decided the time had come for the erection of a semi-foreign bungalow for the Goforths. Since moving to Changte, they had been living in a Chinese house, quite unsuitable for their needs. While their new home was being built the Goforths feared that it might prove a barrier between themselves and the Chinese and perhaps hinder the progress of the work which was going on so hopefully; so they prayed that God would overrule, and not only prevent the new building from being a hindrance, but make it a means of increased blessing to the people. As with so many of their prayers, they came to see that the answer lay in their own hands. A price had to be paid—"open house to all." This price they resolved to pay.
>
> The new home was completed by the fall of 1897. Its architecture was simple, being Chinese in style on the outside while

the interior was like an ordinary bungalow in the homeland. As it was the first building of its kind to be built in that region, the house was naturally an object of great curiosity to the Chinese. The board floors, the glass windows and the shutters, the foreign furniture, the organ, the sewing-machine, (the "iron-tailor" as it was called), even the kitchen stove which let its smoke and gas go out through a chimney instead of into one's eyes and through one's house,—all these were things of wonder to the Chinese. And as for the cellar! Who had ever heard of people having a big hole underneath their house! That must be where the "foreign devils" kept the bodies of the kidnapped children. And so, when it became noised through the district that the foreigners were willing for people to see through their "strange house," multitudes availed themselves of the opportunity.

Goforth led the men through the house in bands of ten or twenty or more at a time, while his wife took charge of the women....

Then Goforth would stand up on the veranda of the house and say, "Men, I have something to tell you. I want you to stand here and listen. If you go roaming about the yard and will not pay attention, I shall not let you see through the house." The house, being the main attraction, they were always ready to listen while Goforth gave a short Gospel address.

Afterwards they were shown through the house. Nothing escaped their curious eyes. Beds were turned back, drawers opened, the sewing-machine examined, the organ played, before they appeared satisfied. We regret to say that a very careful watch had to be kept while leading bands of visitors through. The Chinese had, at that time, great capacious sleeves and they were very dexterous at poking knives, forks, spoons, saucers, pictures and knick-knacks up them. We took what precaution we could, but things would disappear. We found it impossible to keep a pair of foreign-made scissors about the place. Some of the sewing-machine fixtures were taken. One visitor even got away with the carving knife.

Goforth made a special point of allowing them to see the cellar and assisted them in lifting lids off every box and jar and even helped them to turn over the coal, so as to convince them we had nothing to hide from them. This did more than anything else to kill the ugly rumours about the jars of children's flesh that were supposed to be secreted in the cellar.

The high-water mark in visitors received was reached one day in the fall of 1899, when 1,835 men passed through the house. On the same day, Mrs. Goforth received about 500 women.... Goforth had no time to eat dinner that day. His wife handed him a cup of hot milk now and then which kept him going till nightfall....

As can well be imagined, this constant receiving of visitors was exhausting work.

"I have often been receiving and talking to band after band of men in my study from morning right on till evening," wrote Goforth at that time. "About sundown, I sometimes feel so tired that I wish the last had come for today, but I may glance out to the front and there the gatekeeper is bringing in a fresh lot. Am I to say to these men, "I cannot see you today. I am tired. Come some other time." No! How do I know but that the Lord has sent these men specially to me and tired and all as I may be, I bring them in and treat them kindly and tell them of our wonderful Redeemer."

Some missionaries felt that the Goforth's policy of keeping "open house" was a great mistake, that it meant cheapening themselves and the Mission before the people. The future, however, was to reveal abundantly the value of this policy. Deep-seated prejudices were overcome, friendly contacts were made with the highest and of all classes, and many hearts were opened to the Gospel.

"Some may think," writes Goforth, "that receiving visitors is not real Mission work, but I think it is. I put myself out to make friends with the people and I reap the results when I go to their villages to preach. Often the people of a village will gather around me and say, 'We were at your place and you showed us through your house, treating us like friends.' Then they will almost always bring me a chair to sit on, a table to lay my Bible on, and some tea."

Theme

Christians are generous and hospitable
ROMANS 12:13
...contributing to the needs of the saints; given to hospitality.
HEBREWS 13:2
Don't forget to show hospitality to strangers, for in doing so, some have entertained angels without knowing it.

True disciples give one hundred percent to the work of the Kingdom
MATTHEW 25:14-30
He who received the five talents came and brought another five talents, saying, 'Lord, you delivered to me five talents. Behold, I have gained another five talents in addition to them.' "His lord said to him, 'Well done, good and faithful servant. You have been faithful over a few things, I will set you over many things. Enter into the joy of your lord.' (Matthew 25:20-21)

Devotion

The Goforths were concerned that their new semi-Western house could be a hindrance to the relationships with their neighbors. Through prayer they made the decision to open up their private home to locals for sightseeing, which ultimately helped make the work of reaching and evangelizing the people easier, as it made the people see them as friends, not strangers. God honored this sacrifice greatly. Not only did it quell ugly rumors about the missionaries, but when people recognized them later, their hospitality was reciprocated.

Being "on mission," it was natural for the Goforths to view all of their possessions as resources to be spent on the task of winning souls for Christ. Everything large and small, even down to scissors and carving knives, was prayerfully devoted to the larger Kingdom goal. But even more than material things, the Goforths spent the resources of their time and their privacy to come against the strongholds of the enemy. The fundamental sacrifice required was for them to see everything in their hands as entrusted to them by God for His purposes.

Everything we have, whether it was payment for our own labor or an outright gift to us, is ultimately God's provision. In the parable of the talents found in Matthew chapter 25, the faithful servants did not invest a percentage of what was given to them, they invested all of it.

Truly, as followers of Jesus, as His disciples, we are all "on mission."

Reflection

Heavenly Father, please help me to see my time, and everything in my possession, not merely as gifts from Your hand (which they are), but as resources to be invested into other people for the increase of Your Kingdom.

❈

This story begins on page 79 of the Scripture Testimony Edition of *Goforth of China* from Walking Together Press.

Devotion 14: Greater Works Than These

THE Goforths had been through the Boxer Rebellion, where Jonathan nearly lost his life, then they had spent time in Canada on furlough, and now they were back in China to resume their missionary work. But Jonathan was restless. He seemed to see the missionary problem from a wider perspective, and longed for a multiplication of the results.

He was nearing his forty-fifth milestone when a strange restlessness seemed to take possession of him. He dwelt much with his wife on the verse at the head of this chapter, and earnestly he longed to see in his ministry the "greater works" promised. Mr. Goforth had, up to this time, been undoubtedly a successful missionary, judged by ordinary standards, but he himself was never satisfied with what he felt to be "just touching the fringe" of the appalling multitudes needing Christ. His whole soul burned intensely, that our Lord's promise, "and greater works shall ye do," might be fulfilled in him. It might truly be said of Jonathan Goforth that he "delighted to do God's will." His love for the Word amounted to a passion and to learn God's will through the Word was for him to obey at any cost!

We were, as a family, living at one of the out-centers, when some unknown friend in England began sending us pamphlets on the Welsh revival. Scenes of that marvelous movement were vividly described. Eagerly Mr. Goforth looked for these pamphlets, which, for a considerable time, came weekly. While reading them aloud to his wife, he was repeatedly so thrilled and moved that he could scarcely proceed for emotion. A new thought, a new conception, seemed to come to him of God the Holy Spirit and His part in the conviction and conversion of men.

At this time, far off in India, Dr. Margaret McKellar, one with whom we had had most congenial fellowship in the student days of 1887, but had not seen nor corresponded with in the intervening years, was led of God to send Mr. Goforth a little booklet entitled A Great Awakening....

A short time after the booklet had reached us, we returned to our home at Changte and, as the days passed, Mr. Goforth became more and more absorbed in his intensive study of the Holy Spirit. Not that his regular work was ever neglected, but every possible moment, when free to do so, he gave himself to this work, rising before six, sometimes five, in order to get unbroken time at his Bible....

The latter part of the following February, Mr. Goforth left for the great religious fair at Hsunhsien. It was estimated that more than a million pilgrims climbed the hill outside that city during the ten days of the fair for worship of the great image, Lao Nainai (Old Grandmother). This fair was by far the greatest opportunity of the year for reaching numbers with the Gospel and all missionaries and native evangelists possible gathered there for intensive evangelism.

On this particular year, 1906, a great snowstorm had so blocked the roads, few pilgrims had arrived. Goforth therefore decided to use this slack time with the Chinese workers in prayer and preparation, giving them something of what he himself had been receiving.

One evening, while speaking to a heathen audience which filled the street chapel, he witnessed "a stirring in the people's hearts" such as he had never seen before. While speaking on "He bore our sins in His own body on the tree," conviction seemed written on every face. When asking for decisions, practically everyone stood up. Then turning about, seeking for one of the evangelists to take his place, he found the whole band of ten standing in a row with awed looks. One whispered, "Brother, He for whom we have prayed so long, was here in very deed tonight." During the days that followed, at every centre where the Gospel was being proclaimed, men came forward seeking salvation.

Theme

Greater works than these
JOHN 14:12

> Most certainly I tell you, he who believes in me, the works that I do, he will do also; and he will do greater works than these, because I am going to my Father.

Devotion

Jonathan Goforth was, by all measurements, a very successful missionary. But he longed for more. The sheer magnitude of those who did not yet know Christ was staggering, and Goforth felt as if God was calling him to a different phase of ministry, one that would lead to a spiritual awakening that would amplify the spread of the Gospel person to person. This is often termed a "revival" (i.e. believers being revived) which leads to a "spiritual awakening" (i.e. unbelievers being saved in great numbers). Both of these things have occurred throughout history, starting with the Day of Pentecost in the Book of Acts. Both America and the UK have experienced these phenomena many times in the past two hundred fifty years, resulting in mass conversions. Certainly these are some of the "greater things" that Jesus promised.

Jesus said in John 14:12, "Most certainly I tell you, he who believes in me, the works that I do, he will do also; and he will do greater works than these, because I am going to my Father." How could we do greater works than Jesus Himself? He says, "because I am going to my Father." In John 16:7, Jesus tells His disciples, "...I tell you the truth: It is to your advantage that I go away, for if I don't go away, the Counselor won't come to you. But if I go, I will send him to you."

It is through the Holy Spirit that we will accomplish greater works than Jesus, because instead of being in one place at one time, the Spirit of God can be everywhere at once!

Perhaps it was a mid-life crisis. Nonetheless, Jonathan Goforth was restless until he could grab hold of everything God had prepared for him to do. And this leads us to the next book in the *Scripture Testimony Collection*, Jonathan Goforth's *By My Spirit*, which tells story after story of this new work of the Holy Spirit.

Reflection

Do you long for all that God desires for you? Do you believe that through the Holy Spirit we can do even greater works (signs and wonders) than Jesus did when He was here?

※

This story begins on page 127 of the Scripture Testimony Edition of *Goforth of China* from Walking Together Press.

Chapter VIII

By My Spirit

AFTER returning to China, and after escaping the horrible events of the Boxer Rebellion, it seemed like Jonathan Goforth had a personal awakening. He saw the sheer magnitude of the unreached in China with new eyes, and began to be restless for the "even greater works," Jesus promised in John 14:12. At the same time, God led two different people on two different continents to send literature about ongoing revivals in both Wales and India. Deeply stirred by these reports, Mr. Goforth became a student of revivals, both contemporary and historical, which led him to a completely new phase of ministry. For the rest of his missionary career, Jonathan Goforth worked as an evangelist and revivalist. This book is his own astonishing record of the Holy Spirit's work in meeting after meeting, and contains dozens of stories testifying to the reality of God and the truth of His Word.

From the introduction, "But though we speak of the manifestations at Pentecost as being abnormal, yet we maintain that Pentecost was normal Christianity. The results, when the Holy Spirit assumed control in Christ's stead, were according to Divine plan... The purpose

of the Holy Spirit was to glorify the Lord Jesus Christ every day from
the crowning to the coming. It is unthinkable that He should grow
weary in well-doing... Normal Christianity, as planned by our Lord,
was not supposed to begin in the Spirit and continue in the flesh. In
the building of His temple it never was by might nor by power, but
always by His Spirit."

First published in 1929, this Christian classic has been refreshed
with the hope that it will stir the hearts of a new generation, and that
perhaps we will get to experience revivals and awakenings in our own
time. Following are a pair of devotionals based on stories from this
exciting book.

Devotion 15: First Be Reconciled

I n a pattern that would be repeated over and over in the coming
years, for revival to come, repentance must first come personally
within the Christian leaders. Jonathan Goforth had an unresolved
conflict with a fellow missionary that was becoming more and more
of an obstacle, not only to further ministry, but to right relationship
with God.

> In the autumn of 1906, having felt depressed for some time
> by the cold and fruitless condition of my out-stations, I was
> preparing to set out on a tour to see what could be done to revive
> them. There was a matter, however, between the Lord and myself,
> that had to be straightened out before He could use me. I need
> not go into the details. Suffice to say that there was a difference
> between a brother missionary and myself. I honestly felt that I
> was in the right. (Such, of course, is very human. In any difference
> it is always safe to divide by half.) At any rate, the pressure from
> the Spirit was quite plain. It was that I should go and make that
> thing straight. I kept answering back to God that the fault was
> the other man's, not mine; that it was up to him to come to me,
> not for me to go to him.

The pressure continued. "But Lord," I expostulated, "he came to my study and in tears confessed his fault. So, isn't the thing settled?" "You hypocrite!" I seemed to hear Him say, "you know that you are not loving each other as brethren, as I commanded you to." Still I held out. The fault was the other man's, I kept insisting; surely, therefore, I couldn't be expected to do anything about it. Then came the final word, "If you don't straighten this thing out before you go on that trip, you must expect to fail. I can't go with you." That humbled me somewhat. I did not feel at all easy about going on that long and difficult tour without His help. Well I knew that by myself I would be like one beating the air.

The night before I was to start out on my trip I had to lead the prayer-meeting for the Chinese Christians. All the way out to the church the pressure continued: "Go and straighten this thing out, so that I may go with you tomorrow." Still I wouldn't yield. I started the meeting. It was all right while they were singing a hymn and during the reading of Scripture. But as soon as I opened my lips in prayer I became confused, for all the time the Spirit kept saying: "You hypocrite! Why don't you straighten this thing out?" I became still more troubled while delivering the short prayer-address. Finally, when about half-way through my talk the burden became utterly intolerable and I yielded. "Lord," I promised in my heart, "as soon as this meeting is over, I'll go and make that matter right." Instantly something in the audience seemed to snap. My Chinese hearers couldn't tell what was going on in my heart; yet in a moment the whole atmosphere was changed. Upon the meeting being thrown open for prayer, one after another rose to their feet to pray, only to break down weeping. For almost twenty years we missionaries had been working among the Honanese, and had longed in vain to see a tear of penitence roll down a Chinese cheek.

...the difficulty was settled. Next morning, before daybreak, I was on my way to the first out-station. The results of that tour far exceeded anything that I had dared hope for. At each place the spirit of judgment was made manifest. Wrongs were righted and crooked things were made straight. At one place I was only able to spend a single night, but that night all present broke down. In the following year one out-station more than doubled its numbers; to another fifty-four members were added, and to another eighty-eight.

Theme

Be reconciled to your brother before going to the altar
MATTHEW 5:23-24

"If therefore you are offering your gift at the altar, and there remember that your brother has anything against you, leave your gift there before the altar, and go your way. First be reconciled to your brother, and then come and offer your gift.

We will be judged by the same standard
MATTHEW 7:1-5

Why do you see the speck that is in your brother's eye, but don't consider the beam that is in your own eye? Or how will you tell your brother, 'Let me remove the speck from your eye,' and behold, the beam is in your own eye? *You hypocrite!* First remove the beam out of your own eye, and then you can see clearly to remove the speck out of your brother's eye. (Matthew 7:3-5 emphasis added)

Devotion

"You hypocrite!" These are firm words from the Holy Spirit. Jonathan Goforth's experience echoed two passages from the Sermon on the Mount as the Spirit's work in him progressed from gentle teaching to open rebuke.

At first the Lord reasoned with him about the matter of a broken relationship like, "If therefore you are about to leave to conduct revival meetings, and remember that there is unresolved conflict with a brother, you go and make it right before leaving."

When Goforth wouldn't listen, the Holy Spirit allowed him to see how his attitude would hinder the ministry, as if He was saying, "Why do you see the unconfessed sin in the congregation, but don't consider this sinful unresolved conflict in your own heart? *You hypocrite!* First confess your own sin and repent, and then I will pour out the spirit of repentance on the congregation."

An earlier devotion (Devotion 8: The Burning Hot Coin) is based on a story from Hudson Taylor in which he also felt like a hypocrite. We saw how he faced a watershed moment in his faith. Taylor believed that a specific obedience to the leading of the Spirit set him on a lifelong path of faith in God's provision. Likewise for Jonathan Goforth, it seemed that God was setting before him a choice, to go forward in ministry with God's strength, or in his own strength. For Hudson Taylor the test involved the giving of his last coin, while for Goforth it meant humbling himself and seeking reconciliation with a brother. Praise God that we get to read of the lifetimes of glorious fruit that resulted from these moments of testing in these two men's lives.

Having yielded to the conviction of the Holy Spirit in his own life, and having personally experienced the resulting freedom and lightness of heart, Goforth was able to freely pray for others to receive this blessing.

Reflection

Each follower of Jesus is like a tool in His toolbelt of ministry. Perhaps there is a hurting person who has just cried out in prayer for help, so God looks in His toolbelt for one of His servants to render aid. He pulls one out, but notices that the edge is quite dull, being blunted by unconfessed sin or unresolved conflicts.

Is there some broken relationship in your life that you could do more to make right? Has the Spirit been reminding you of this and its hindrance to the ministry God has for you? Go and be reconciled, and therefore become a sharpened tool in God's toolbelt, ready to be used in the hands of the Master craftsman.

❦

This story begins on page 13 of the Scripture Testimony Edition of *By My Spirit* from Walking Together Press.

Devotion 16: Simply Because They Prayed

JONATHAN Goforth had been reading voraciously about revivals that were occurring both in Wales and in India, but so far he had not yet experienced anything like these reports described. But then, an opportunity opened up for him to visit nearby Korea where great revival had just begun.

It was only a few months after I had completed this tour that the religious world was electrified by the marvelous story of the Korean Revival. The Foreign Mission Secretary of our Church, Dr. R. P. MacKay, who was visiting in China at the time, asked me to accompany him to Korea. I need hardly say how greatly I rejoiced at such an opportunity. The Korean movement was of incalculable significance in my life because it showed me at first-hand the boundless possibilities of the revival method. It is one thing to read about Revival in books. To witness its working with one's own eyes and to feel its atmosphere with one's own heart is a different thing altogether. Korea made me feel, as it did many others, that this was God's plan for setting the world aflame.

I had not been in Korea very long before I was led back to the source from which this great movement sprang. Mr. Swallen, of

Pingyang, told me how that the missionaries of his station, both Methodists and Presbyterians, upon hearing of the great Revival in the Kassia Hills of India, had decided to pray every day at the noon hour until a similar blessing was poured out upon them. "After we had prayed for about a month," said Mr. Swallen, "a brother proposed that we stop the prayer-meeting, saying, 'We have been praying now for a month, and nothing unusual has come of it. We are spending a lot of time. I don't think we are justified. Let us go on with our work as usual, and each pray at home is he finds it convenient.' The proposal seemed plausible. The majority of us, however, decided that, instead of discontinuing the prayer meeting, we would give more time to prayer, not less. With that in view, we changed the hour from noon to four o'clock; we were then free to pray until supper-time, if we wished. We kept to it, until at last, after months of waiting, the answer came."

As I remember, those missionaries at Pingyang were just ordinary, every-day people. I did not notice any outstanding figure among them. They seemed to live and work and act like other missionaries. It was in prayer that they were different. One evening, Dr. MacKay and myself were invited to attend the missionary prayer-meeting. Never have I been so conscious of the Divine Presence as I was that evening. Those missionaries seemed to carry us right up to the very Throne of God. One had the feeling that they were indeed communing with God, face to face. On the way back to our host's residence, Dr. MacKay was silent for some time. I could see that he was greatly agitated. Finally, with deep emotion, he exclaimed: "What amazing prayer! You missionaries in Honan are nowhere near that high level."

What impressed me, too, was the practical nature of the movement. I soon saw that this was no wild gust of "religious enthusiasm," dying with the wind upon whose wings it had been borne. There were, of course, the usual outward manifestations which inevitably accompany such phenomenal outpourings of spiritual power. But beyond all that was the simple fact that here were tens of thousands of Korean men and women whose lives had been completely transformed by the touch of the Divine fire. I saw great churches, seating fifteen hundred people, so crowded that it was found necessary to hold two services, one for the men and one for the women. Everyone seemed almost pathetically eager to spread the "glad tidings." Even little boys would run up to people on the street and plead with them to accept Christ as their Savior. One thing that especially struck me was their abounding liberality. The poverty of the Koreans is proverbial. Yet one missionary told me that he was afraid to speak to them about money; they were giving so much already. Everywhere I saw an evident devotion for the Holy Word. Everyone seemed to carry a Bible. And permeating it all was that marvellous spirit of prayer.

Theme

All great movements of God are birthed in prayer

ACTS 1:14

> All these with one accord continued steadfastly in prayer and supplication, along with the women, and Mary the mother of Jesus, and with his brothers.

ACTS 4:31

> When they had prayed, the place was shaken where they were gathered together. They were all filled with the Holy Spirit, and they spoke the word of God with boldness.

Devotion

Revival is a movement of God, without a doubt. In the preceding verses from Acts, we see two events that resulted in powerful waves of the Holy Spirit, which in turn resulted in bold proclamations of the Gospel as well as bold expressions of the blessings of Kingdom life. But take note of the common elements. It is clear from these verses, and from myriad stories represented in the *Scripture Testimony Collection,* that revival is fundamentally an answer to prayer.

How long should we expect to pray for things that are already in God's will? How long do we pray for a wayward child? How long do we pray for provision? George Müller once prayed for a specific need for18 months, ten days.* How long do we need to pray for revival?

Perhaps the principle is to pray past the point of wanting to give up? The "ordinary, every-day" people in Pingyang** prayed at least twice as long after some had wanted to give up. Then, "...at last, after months of waiting, the answer came." And even after the revival blessing was being poured out, they continued in a "marvellous spirit of prayer."

Reflection

Heavenly Father, we are ordinary people with ordinary doubts and ordinary discouragements. Please help us to have faith to be patient in prayer, and to trust You for the extraordinary.

❦

This story begins on page 15 of the Scripture Testimony Edition of *By My Spirit* from Walking Together Press.

---

* Devotion 2: The Answer is Yet to Come
** Today it is the capital of North Korea and is called Pyongyang

Devotion 17: Divinely Directed Donkey

V ILLAGE after village was experiencing revival as a sustained
wave of the Spirit swept through the region. It appeared that
conviction, tears, and repentance were contagious leading to
widespread joy and worship. Even a notorious gambler was caught
up in the wave, though in a most unusual way.

At another village in the same region there was a certain notorious character who was renowned far and wide for his phenomenal success at the gambling table. One day this man saddled his
donkey and, started up north to collect some money from certain
of his victims who lived in that direction. But he got no further
than the outskirts of the village when the donkey stopped. The
gambler kicked and beat and cursed it, but all to no avail. The
animal was adamant. North it would not go. Then it occurred to
the man that there were some villages to the south where money
was owing him. So he turned the donkey around and it started off
without any trouble. Everything ran smoothly enough until they
came to a cross-road where one branch went south-east and one
south-west. The gambler had in mind a village which lay along the
road running south-west. It was upon that road, therefore, that he

endeavoured to urge his steed. But again the donkey had decided differently. It made quite clear to its master that if it were to budge another inch the route followed must be the one running south-east. Blows and entreaties were alike of none effect. "All right, have your own way," said the man at last, disgustedly, "and anyway, if I am not mistaken, there are some who owe me money down that way, too." So they proceeded on their journey.

In a little while they came to a village. They continued up the main street until they were directly opposite a little Christian church. Here the donkey stopped, and nothing the man could do could make it move a foot farther. In despair the man alighted. Now it happened that some of the Christians who had attended the Liaoyang meetings were holding a service in the church. The gambler, standing non-plussed outside the door, heard the sound of singing. His curiosity aroused, he decided to enter and see what it was all about. The power of God was present there that day. He heard this one, in tears, confessing his sins, and that one, with radiant face, telling of the joy and peace that had come into his life. Soon a powerful conviction came over the man. He stood up and confessed his sins and told how he had been led to the meeting. "How can I help but know," he cried, "that this is the voice of God?"

Theme

God using circumstances and timing to communicate
ACTS 11:11
> Behold, immediately three men stood before the house where I was, having been sent from Caesarea to me.

Devotion

In Acts chapter 11, the Apostle Peter is telling his skeptical friends about a series of events through which God clearly told him something extremely important. From a thrice-repeated heavenly vision, to hearing both the voice and the inner urging of the Holy Spirit, to the perfect timing of circumstances, Peter is convinced to go with some Gentiles and initiate the spread of the Gospel to the rest of the world.

What is so special about three men coming to a house to ask for Peter? In itself, not much. But three men coming "immediately" after God spoke in multiple ways to Peter, showed him that the arrival of the men was also God's "voice."

Donkeys are known to be stubborn animals, and it is not unusual for one to stop randomly, perhaps requiring the rider to dismount and try to urge the animal onward. But considering the events that unfolded for the gambler, it was clear in retrospect that the donkey's resolve was not random. As the former gambler said, "How can I help but know that this is the voice of God?"

Reflection

More often than not, it seems that divinely orchestrated circumstances are identified after the fact. The gambler didn't think much of his donkey's stubbornness until later, when it became profound.

Can you identify the finger of God in some seemingly ordinary circumstance in your life? If so, take a moment to thank Him, and then tell the story to someone else. You will build both your faith and theirs!

※

This story begins on page 25 of the Scripture Testimony Edition of *By My Spirit* from Walking Together Press.

Chapter IX

Chinese Diamonds for the King of Kings

Have you ever heard of someone described as a jewel? "What a dear old saint! He is such a jewel." The truth is that every person, since he or she is uniquely made by God, is a jewel in His eyes. If we take the time to learn a person's story, we can see their gem-like qualities too.

Jonathan and Rosalind Goforth encountered beautiful soul after beautiful soul, and these delightful vignettes of transforming grace are gleaned from their personal experiences in China. These stories of redemption and refinement reveal human gem stones set apart *for the King of Kings.* God is able to do the miraculous, bringing the lowly opium addict up from the dirt, or the proud scholar down from his pedestal, transforming them both into brothers and sisters—peers—in the Kingdom family. Story after story in this small book testify to the reality of God and the truth of His word.

From the foreword, "Whole libraries have been written on Christian evidences. The resources of philosophic and scientific research have been drawn up in defence of the Christian faith. Yet important as these are, it may be questioned whether any or all of them together bring home to the heart such conviction as does the story of a redeemed soul—a soul lifted out of the fearful pit and miry clay—cleansed, purified and established in righteousness. Whatever intellectual difficulties may occur, a countenance illumined with a light that is not of this world is irresistible."

From the introduction, "The little book is sent forth with the earnest hope and prayer that those who read these sketches may come to see the truth of what Paul said: 'God hath made of ONE BLOOD all men under heaven.'"

Following are two devotions from stories in *Chinese Diamonds for the King of Kings* by Rosalind Goforth.

Devotion 18: Dead to Sin, Alive to God

D RUG addiction is a terrible demon that sadly holds many in its grip until their destruction. But it can have no grasp on a dead person, as can be seen by the following story about poor Wang Fu Lin, who had been a hopeless opium addict...until he was dead.

"Call upon me in the day of trouble and I will deliver thee, and thou shalt glorify me."

A poor broken opium slave lay on a kang or brick bed with only a thin straw mat between his emaciated form and the cold bricks. His livid color, with the peculiar dark shade of the moderate opium user, his sunken cheeks and labored breathing, all betokened the man had reached the stage when only a miracle could save him. Beside him stood a missionary, who was saying earnestly as he laid his hand kindly on the man's shoulder:

"Wang Fu Lin, I tell you God can save you."

"No, no, Pastor," the man replied sadly, "It's no use. I've tried and failed too often. I believe all you preach, but what is the use of believing when this opium binds me as with iron chains? Even Pastor Hsi's Refuge failed to cure me. No no, don't waste your time on me. I'm beyond hope." And the man turned again to his opium.

But the missionary was not the kind to be so easily rebuffed. The next day found Wang Fu Lin and the missionary on the Mission court en route for the station of Chu Wang.

For ten awful days Wang Fu Lin's body, mind and soul hung in the balance. The missionaries united in doing all that was possible to relieve the man's agonies. It was on the tenth night the crisis came. Many times later Wang Fu Lin told how that night he went out when in bitter agony into the darkness. To his distorted brain there appeared to him a horrible being urging him to jump the wall and get relief once more in opium. As he stood wavering a voice seemed to call to him, "Wang Fu Lin, Wang Fu Lin, beware! Yield now and you are lost." As he heard this voice he made one desperate effort, crying aloud, "Oh, God, help me. I will die rather than yield." Staggering back to his brick bed he threw himself upon it and slept till morning. He wakened, as the future proved, a new and victorious man.

Theme

Disciples are dead to sin and self, and alive to God
ROMANS 6:5-11

For if we have become united with him in the likeness of his death, we will also be part of his resurrection; knowing this, that our old man was crucified with him, that the body of sin might be done away with, so that we would no longer be in bondage to sin. *For he who has died has been freed from sin.* But if we died with Christ, we believe that we will also live with him; knowing that Christ, being raised from the dead, dies no more. Death no longer has dominion over him! For the death that he died, he died to sin one time; but the life that he lives, he lives to God. *Thus consider yourselves also to be dead to sin, but alive to God in Christ Jesus our Lord.* (emphasis added)

Devotion

When talking about those trapped in addiction we often hear phrases like, "He has to hit rock bottom," or "She must come to the end of herself." This is true, but then what?

Picture the addict as a person on a little boat in a raging sea. The boat is a bit of relative comfort compared to being lost in the sea, but even if the boat is not dashed to pieces, staying there will mean loneliness and eventually starving to death. That the addict must get out of the boat is obvious, but to where? What is there to stand on in the awful tumult except the false hope of the little boat?

Wang Fu Lin had reached the point of total resignation. He simply *had* to get out. He was willing to step out of the boat even if it meant death. But at the same time he did the one thing that saves us all. With all his heart, he cried aloud, "Oh, God, help me." As he figuratively stepped out of the boat into a certain watery death, just before he sank beneath the waves, a Mighty Hand pulled him to life.

The reality is that this is a picture of each one of us. We may not be addicted to a drug, but we are certainly addicted to ourselves. In our proud self-sufficiency, we rebuff the outstretched arms of God saying, "No, I'm fine. I've got this." Until we don't.

George Müller, that famous, mighty man of faith, had to come to the end of himself before he could experience life in Christ Jesus, and then go on to blessing countless others from the richness of that life.

> To one who asked [George Müller] the secret of his service he said: "There was a day when I died, utterly died;" and, as he spoke, he bent lower and lower until he almost touched the floor—"died to George Müller, his opinions, preferences, tastes and will—died to the world, its approval or censure—died to the approval or blame even of my brethren and friends—and since then I have studied only to show myself approved unto God."*

---

* Pierson, Arthur T. 2023. *George Müller of Bristol (Scripture Testimony Edition)*. Estes Park: Walking Together Press. pg. 239

Reflection

For he who has died has been freed from sin. But if we died with Christ, *we believe that we will also live with him...* Thus consider yourselves also to be dead to sin, *but alive to God in Christ Jesus our Lord.*

This story begins on page 30 of the Scripture Testimony Edition of *Chinese Diamonds for the King of Kings* from Walking Together Press.

Devotion 19: Seeing Christ in Them

M R. Wang had been hired as a private language tutor for a missionary that was learning to speak Chinese. But fearing the scandalous reputation of the missionaries (they supposedly ate children, for example), he fled. In time, and as the natural pressures of a lack of employment increased, he regretted his decision to leave. He resolved that if the opportunity should come again, he would gladly take the teaching position. And that opportunity did come.

...Mr. Wang, making a low bow hurriedly asked forgiveness in a few humble words. He ended by saying, "I know, sir, you are not what people say you are. I was wrong, forgive me. If you will take me back I will be glad to teach you."

While he was speaking the missionary's face was a study—surprise, annoyance, relief, pleasure—all came in turn. The missionary, who could now speak the Chinese language a little, laid his hand kindly on the young man's shoulder and said:

"Not a word more, Mr. Wang. I am in need of a teacher so you may consider yourself engaged, but you must be ready to start back with us three days from now."

The poor fellow looked his gratitude but could find no words. As he turned to leave the missionary called him back and said in a low voice as he handed him some money, "Take this, you have a wife and she must be provided for, we will reckon later." This thoughtful act completed the capture of Mr. Wang's heart. From that moment he became the devoted follower of the missionary although as yet he knew nothing of his message.

Three days later found Mr. Wang settled in his little "tsang" or cabin on the missionary's houseboat. Next to his was the larger cabin occupied by the two missionaries as sleeping and living apartment. A partition of open woodwork covered with paper separated the two cabins. Mr. Wang had not been in his compartment very long before he had, in true Chinese fashion, by moistening the tip of his finger and applying it to the paper partition, made a hole sufficiently large to enable him to watch all that passed in the adjoining cabin without himself being seen. Day by day he spent every moment he could get at his self made vantage ground. How those men puzzled him! As he noticed how quiet and orderly, and above all how strangely happy they were, without being boisterous, he became conscious of a growing sense of respect and admiration. Before they had reached their destination, the missionary's home, Mr. Wang had lost every trace of doubt or fear of the foreigners.

Mr. ——, the missionary, was a keen judge of character. His knowledge of human nature was gained in the slums of a so-called Christian city, and it was well for him that such experience had been gained before meeting the more complex problems of the Chinese character. As day by day the missionary studied with Mr. Wang he became more and more convinced that this man must meet Christ first in him, His representative, for he found him sharp, keen, critical, and alas, utterly untrustworthy. But the day came when Mr. Wang testified, when he was being received into the Church, "I learned first to love the Pastor, then to love his Saviour."

Theme

Believers are ambassadors for Christ
2 CORINTHIANS 5:18-21

> We are therefore ambassadors on behalf of Christ, as though God were entreating by us: we beg you on behalf of Christ, be reconciled to God. (2 Corinthians 5:20)

Devotion

Mr. Wang closely observed—even to the point of spying on—the missionaries by whom he was employed as a language teacher. He was greatly puzzled by these men, at how quiet and orderly they were, and above all, how strangely happy they were. His respect and admiration grew until he finally realized that he was seeing Christ in them.

My own testimony is similar to Mr. Wang's. I did not grow up in a Christian home, and while I knew people who went to church, I am not sure that I had ever met a true follower of Jesus. When I was fifteen years old, I got a job in a bicycle shop called Spirit Cycle Works. The telephone number was 541-LORD. (These little clues, like so many Christian bumper stickers, were lost on me.)

The guys at the bike shop were Christians, but they did not talk to me overtly about God. They did not ask the classic questions like, "Do you believe in God?" or "Where will you go after you die?" or "Do you know Jesus?" Instead, they just became my friends. We worked together, laughed together, and rode bicycles together for hundreds of miles. All the while, I saw powerfully attractive qualities in them that I could not explain. And I would listen to their conversations, which were full of the Kingdom of God, for example, "Yeah, this difficult thing happened, but this is how God met us in it. He brought resolution and healing and joy into the situation."

After about six months one of the guys said, "Hey, we have a Bible study on Tuesday evenings. Would you like to come?" I readily agreed to attend. That evening I walked into a house full of probably thirty people who all had that attractive quality. I asked what it was, to which they said, "Oh! That's Jesus!"

That evening I said yes to Jesus. Like Mr. Wang, I learned first to love my friends, and then I learned to love their Savior, because I had seen and met Him through His ambassadors.

While I did not spy on my coworkers like Mr. Wang, I watched them very closely. Six months of working together almost every day allowed me to witness them go through both good days and bad days. I saw that they didn't merely have beliefs about God, they knew Him, walked with Him, *trusted Him,* and were full to overflowing with His Spirit. They loved each other, and they loved me!

Reflection

Jesus said that His disciples would be salt and light to those around them. (Matthew 5:13-16) He is not telling us to order our behavior so that we look good in the eyes of others. Rather He is pointing out that others are always observing us, even when we may not notice.

This story begins on page 101 of the Scripture Testimony Edition of *Chinese Diamonds for the King of Kings* from Walking Together Press.

Chapter X

How I Know God Answers Prayer

ALL of the books in the *Scripture Testimony Collection* are in the public domain, which means that they are all around one hundred years old, or more. At that time in history, the debate between religion and science—and the notion that they are contradictory—was on the rise in popular culture. Supposedly educated and sophisticated people simply don't believe in prayer.

Both *Answered or Unanswered?* and *Chinese Diamonds for the King of Kings* address this topic directly in their introductory material, while the title of Rosalind Goforth's book, *How I Know God Answers Prayer,* is her emphatic statement on the topic.

During the course of this nearly fifty years of ministry the Goforths experienced God's direct involvement through the miraculous transformation of souls, through His generous and timely provision for their needs, and through dramatic deliverance from disease, from persecution, and from violence during the 1900 Boxer Rebellion. All of these things were the direct result of prayer and trust. They even got a peek into God's ways when they would learn of the correlation between a great need and someone on the other side of the world being strongly compelled to pray.

How I Know God Answers Prayer is a collection of the Goforth's personal testimonies to answered prayer. From the Foreword, "It was at the close of the 1908-10 furlough—during which, as a family, we had been blessed with many and, to our weak faith, wonderful answers to prayer—that my oldest son urged me to put down in some definite form the answers to prayer of my life, and extracted from me a solemn promise that I would do so. But months passed after returning to China, and the record had not been touched. Then came a sudden and serious illness which threatened my life, when the doctor told me I must not delay in getting my affairs in order. It was then that an overwhelming sense of regret took possession of me that I had not set down the prayer testimonies, and solemnly I covenanted with the Lord that if he would raise me up they should be written."

Devotion 20: The Perfect Man for the Job

JONATHAN and Rosalind Goforth were feeling the strain of being
stretched too thin. While opportunities multiplied, with glorious
fruit resulting, they would spend nine to ten hours per day hosting,
talking, visiting, and preaching. Then they would have the regular
responsibilities of day to day life and keeping house with their small
children.

> One day Mr. Goforth came to me with his Bible open at the
> promise, "My God shall supply all your need," and asked: "Do
> we believe this? If we do, then God can and will supply us with
> some one to help preach to these crowds, if we ask in faith."
> He prayed very definitely for a man to preach. With my doubt-
> blinded heart, I thought it was as if he were asking for rain from
> a clear sky. Yet, even while he prayed, God was moving one to
> come to us. A day or two later there appeared at the mission the
> converted opium fiend, Wang Fu-Lin, whose conversion has been
> already recorded. [See Devotion 18: Dead to Sin, Alive to God]
> No one could have looked less like the answer to our prayers
> than he did. Fearfully emaciated from long years of excessive
> opium smoking, racked with a cough which three years later

---

ended his life, dressed in such filthy rags as only a beggar would wear, he presented a pitiable sight. Yet the Lord seeth not as man seeth.

After consulting together Mr. Goforth decided to try him for a few days, believing that he could at least testify to the power of God to save a man from his opium. Soon he was reclothed in some of my husband's Chinese garments; and within an hour or two of his entering the mission gate, practically a beggar, he was seated in charge of the men's chapel, so changed one could scarcely have recognized him.

From the first day of his ministry at Changte there was no doubt in the minds of any who heard him that he had indeed been sent to us by our gracious God, for he had in a remarkable degree the unction and power of the Holy Ghost. His gifts as a speaker were all consecrated to one object—the winning of souls to Jesus Christ. He seemed conscious that his days were few, and always spoke as a dying man to dying men. Little wonder is it, therefore, that from the very beginning of his ministry in our chapel men were won to Christ. God spared him to us for the foundation laying of the church at Changte, then called him higher.

Theme

God's work will not lack God's supply
PHILIPPIANS 4:19
My God will supply every need of yours according to his riches in glory in Christ Jesus.

Devotion

The Goforths were already accustomed to asking and then trusting God for material provision such as food, clothing, or money. But to ask for people? Why not? The Apostle Paul said that his God will supply *every need of yours*. This is the first principle.

The second principle is from Matthew chapter 7, in which Jesus says, "Who among you, if his son asks for a fish, will give him a stone? ...If you then, being evil, know how to give good gifts to your children, how much more will your Father in heaven give you what is good?"

It is so great how Jesus does not say, "How much more will your Father in heaven give you fish?" i.e. the thing that was requested. Instead, He says that the Father will give what is good, with the implication that our Father knows what is truly good even better than we.

God wonderfully answered their prayer for a helper in Wang Fu-Lin, whom God had clearly prepared for the work. Although at first Wang Fu-Lin was probably more like a stone than a fish to the surprised Goforths.

Reflection

According to the Lord's Prayer (Matthew 6), we are to first pray for the coming of His Kingdom, then we are to pray for our daily bread. As we are devoted to the Kingdom mission, we can be assured that "... God will supply every need of yours (though maybe not exactly as we imagine) according to his riches in glory in Christ Jesus."

⚜

This story begins on page 24 of the Scripture Testimony Edition of *How I Know God Answers Prayer* from Walking Together Press.

Devotion 21: Prayer of Faith for the Sick

THE Goforths were Presbyterian missionaries from Canada. Presbyterians are typically viewed as "cessationists," and believe that the miraculous signs and wonders we read about in the Book of Acts ceased after the original Apostles passed away. While there are instances in history of charismatic movements amongst the Presbyterians, the Goforths were not among them, and they generally shunned emotionalism. And yet, they had the utmost faith in God. They knew He delights to answer prayer, even prayer that might be outside their theological box.

I had been holding a class for women at an out-station, staying in the home of the elder, Dr. Fan. The day before I was to return home, Mrs. Fan asked me to go with her to visit a very sick boy whom the missionary doctor had sent home from the boys' school, Wei Hwei, because of his having tuberculosis of the lungs. Mrs. Fan told me the mother was in great distress, and begged me to come and pray with her. I found the lad in a truly pitiable condition. His mouth was swollen, his face a ghastly hue, and every moment a cough racked his frame. He seemed to me quite beyond hope, and looked as if he could not live long.

116

On our way home to Mrs. Fan's, the message of James 5:14, 15, kept coming persistently to me, as if spoken by a voice: "Is any sick among you? let him call for the elders of the church; and let them pray over him, ...and the prayer of faith shall save the sick, and the Lord shall raise him up."

I simply could not get away from those words. On reaching Dr. Fan's home, I sent for him, and asked if he and the other elders would be willing to pray with me over the lad. He consented, though at first he seemed rather dubious. There were quite a number of Christians gathered around as we placed the boy in our midst. All knelt down, and I read the words from James. I told them plainly that I could not say that it was indeed the Lord's will to heal the boy; all that was clear to me was that we must obey as far as we had light, and leave the rest in God's hands for life or death. Several prayed, and we then dispersed.

Early the following morning I left for home. Circumstances prevented my return to that place, and in time we moved to another field. More than two years later, while visiting Wei Hwei, I met Mrs. Fan, who told me that the lad had completely recovered and was then working with his father. Still a year later I met Dr. Fan, and upon inquiring about the lad, the doctor told me he was perfectly well, and was in business in Wei Hwei City.

Theme

Prayer of faith for the sick
JAMES 5:14-15

> Is any among you sick? Let him call for the elders of the assembly, and let them pray over him, anointing him with oil in the name of the Lord, and the prayer of faith will heal him who is sick, and the Lord will raise him up. If he has committed sins, he will be forgiven.

Devotion

Theologians for centuries have tried to avoid the plain meaning of James 5:14-15. Some have tried to spiritualize it, making it about salvation and healing the soul. While some have tried to explain that it was only applicable for Apostolic times, and no longer applies to modern times. It is not clear how the Goforths interpreted the passage, but the way she writes makes it seem like miraculous healing was not her first thought, and she mentions that Dr. Fan "seemed rather dubious."

But the Goforths were people of faith, having experienced innumerable answers to prayer, and witnessed countless miraculous transformations of sinners into saints. They also walked closely with God, such that they were able to recognize His voice. This time, He was practically yelling James 5:14-15 to Rosalind Goforth. She "simply could not get away from those words."

> "...all that was clear to me was that we must obey as far as we had light..."

And so, in obedience and faith, they prayed for the sick child, and left the rest in God's hands.

Reflection

So far in these devotions we have seen many hard choices made; Hudson Taylor giving his last coin, Jonathan Goforth humbling himself to reconcile, and now Rosalind Goforth obeying the plain reading of the Scripture on behalf of a dying boy.

Are you willing to do anything that God may call you to do?

❈

This story begins on page 85 of the Scripture Testimony Edition of *How I Know God Answers Prayer* from Walking Together Press.

Chapter XI

Sadhu Sundar Singh

SUNDAR Singh was raised in a home in India that was religious to a degree not comprehensible to the modern Western mind-set. His prominent family followed the Sikh religion, with his mother being the spiritual leader. She taught young Sundar to pursue God, as understood by the Sihks, with all his being, and to seek the truth wherever it may be found, leading to a respect for other religions in so far as they too are seeking truth. Each of his days were full of routine religious devotions both by himself, and with his beloved mother.

Then it all came crashing down.

Sundar lost both his mother and an older brother in a short amount of time. His spiritual center was dead and he was cast adrift. At the same time, he had been attending a Christian school. While his family appreciated the quality education, Sundar saw and hated the cultural imperialism of the West. In his mind, Christianity was merely an extension of it. His resentment boiled over into full-blown hatred after the death of his mother. He began to persecute Christians, becoming a ringleader of youths who would hurl stones at evangelists in the market, but he found no peace in these actions. Then he shocked everyone, including his own family, by publicly burning a New Testament. But he found no peace in this either. In fact, his angst only increased.

Finally, in this time of profound personal crisis, in which his lifetime of intense spiritual devotion still offered no peace, Sundar Singh was defeated and determined to kill himself if he could not find the True God. Half an hour before the appointed time with the deadly train track, he had a vision of Jesus Christ, the one who saves. This encounter forever changed Sundar Singh and set him on the path of being a Christian Sadhu, or holy man, who—with "neither purse, nor scrip"—walked barefoot from village to village and over mountain passes to Tibet, preaching the Good News of Jesus Christ.

In the ultimate expression of cultural adaptation, Sundar Singh's lifestyle as a Sadhu brought the Gospel of Jesus directly to the Indian people, without all the distracting and harmful Western trappings. Archbishop Söderblom wrote, "Here is an Indian soul, who has remained as genuinely Indian as possible, in the best meaning of the word, while becoming absorbed in the love of Christ and completely accepting the Gospel. It would not be easy to find anyone... who has more thoroughly assimilated the Gospel to himself than Sundar Singh. What is typical about him is not a fusion of Christianity and Hinduism, but a fresh presentation of Biblical Christianity that is in many ways stimulating and illuminating for ourselves."

Sadhu Sundar Singh's life of simple faith in—and total devotion to—his Master impacted millions, not only in India, but all over the world. In addition to his annual treks over the mountains on the Hindustan-Tibet Road, he had the opportunity to preach to huge audiences in Europe, America, and Asia. Although he did not have kind words for the materialistic lifestyles of Western Christians, he was able to point people to Jesus, away from their idols, toward lives of total devotion; thereby strengthening their faith.

Many books have been written about Sadhu Sundar Singh, some by himself, and many by those who knew him and were profoundly influenced by him. *Sadhu Sundar Singh, A Personal Memoir* was written by one of Sundar Singh's intimate friends, and is one of the amazing, *must-read* titles in the Scripture Testimony Collection.

Author Charles Freer Andrews was many things; Anglican priest, missionary, educator, social reformer, and activist. He was one of Mahatma Gandhi's closest friends, having the intimacy to use Gandhi's first name, *Mohan*. In turn, Gandhi nicknamed C. F. Andrews *Christ's Faithful Apostle*, based on his initials. Another of C. F. Andrews' intimate friends was Sadhu Sundar Singh, and it is from that friendship that his intimate memoir of Singh has been written. From the last chapter, "The constant remembrance of [Sundar Singh], during all these intervening years, has brought me nearer to Christ. When I was with him in the Himalayas and at Delhi, as this memoir will show, he strengthened my own faith and helped me to keep the pure flame of Christ's love burning bright. Therefore, it has been my one great longing that the reading of this book may be the means of passing on to others that same devotion to Christ."

Following are two Scriptural devotions drawn from passages in the book, *Sadhu Sundar Singh, A Personal Memoir,* newly re-released from Walking Together Press.

Devotion 22: A Damascus Road Experience

Like the Apostle Paul, Sundar Singh had undergone a lifetime of rigorous religious training, which focused not only on seeking truth, but in *living it out*. When personal crisis and his anger against Christianity drove him to more and more violent actions, he became increasingly conflicted. His conscience bothered him. Were these the kinds of actions his mother had taught him? Was this what it looked like to live out truth? What was truth? *Who* was Truth? Hoping to assuage his burning conscience, his religious zeal drove him to one more act...

This form of violence in action, which was alien to his nature, came to a head in the middle of December, 1903, when Sundar brought into his father's courtyard a copy of the Christian Gospels and set fire to it in public. Such a public burning of a sacred religious book was an event unheard of before in the village of Rampur.

"Though," he wrote, "according to my own ideas at that time, I thought that I had done a good deed in burning the Gospel, yet my unrest of heart increased, and for the two following days I was very miserable. On the third day, when I could bear it no longer, I got up at three in the morning and prayed that if there was a God at all He would reveal Himself to me."

What followed formed the greatest turning-point in all his life. It must be given in his own words.

"My intention was," he said, "that if I got no satisfaction, I would place my head upon the railway-line when the five o'clock train passed by and kill myself. If I got no satisfaction in this life, I thought I would get it in the next. I was praying and praying but received no answer; and I prayed for half an hour longer hoping to get peace. At 4.30 a.m. I saw something of which I had no idea previously. In the room where I was praying I saw a great light. I thought the place was on fire. I looked round but could find nothing. The thought came to me that this might be an answer that God had sent me. Then as I prayed and looked into the light, I saw the form of the Lord Jesus Christ. It had such an appearance of glory and love! If it had been some Hindu incarnation I would have prostrated myself before it. But it was the Lord Jesus Christ, whom I had been insulting a few days before.

"I felt that a vision like this could not come out of my own imagination. I heard a voice saying in Hindustani: 'How long will you persecute me? I have come to save you; you were praying to know the right way. Why do you not take it?' So I fell at His feet and got this wonderful peace, which I could not get anywhere else. This was the joy I was wishing to get. This was heaven itself.

"When I got up, the vision had all disappeared; but although the vision disappeared, the peace and joy have remained with me ever since.

Theme

Jesus reveals Himself to an unbeliever
ACTS 9:4-7

> He fell on the earth, and heard a voice saying to him, "Saul, Saul, why do you persecute me?" He said, "Who are you, Lord?" The Lord said, "I am Jesus, whom you are persecuting...." (Acts 9:4-5)

Blessed are those who have not seen and yet have believed
JOHN 20:26-29
> Jesus said to him, "Because you have seen me, you have believed. Blessed are those who have not seen, and have believed." (John 20:29)

I PETER 1:8-9
> ...whom, not having known, you love. In him, though now you don't see him, yet believing, you rejoice greatly with joy that is unspeakable and full of glory, receiving the result of your faith, the salvation of your souls.

Devotion

Very much like the Apostle Paul, Jesus appeared to Sundar Singh asking, "How long will you persecute me?" This experience of Sundar Singh's is not unique to him and the Apostle Paul. Jesus has appeared to many unbelieving people, in many cultures, even in the twentieth and twenty-first centuries.* But this begs the question of why He hasn't appeared to all of us, or at least to more of us. It also begs the question of why He is so silent and hidden to most of us. There is another well-known Christian who asked these very questions.

Corrie ten Boom, known to some as charming "double-old-grandmother," is best known for her deliverance from Ravensbrück, the World War II Nazi death camp, after which she spent more than thirty years traveling the world as a writer and public speaker telling about the love of God. She is famous for repeating everywhere the words of her sister Betsy, before she died in the concentration camp, "There is no pit so deep that He is not deeper still."

In 1922 when Corrie ten Boom was a young woman, she had the opportunity to hear Sadhu Sundar Singh speak at a weekend conference in the Netherlands. She later cited him as a person who

---

* At the time of this writing, there are thirty-two stories about Jesus appearing to a non-believer in the *Scripture Testimony Index* at https://walkingtogether.life, and more will surely be added as the data science research project at Walking Together Press continues.

had influenced her life, but at first, his story was hard for Corrie to hear.

> That weekend, as I listened to the Sadhu, I was amazed but disturbed. He told of the visions he had seen—of how he really saw Jesus—at a time when he didn't believe. We had all read about the Apostle Paul's experiences on the road to Damascus, but here was a man who claimed to have had this experience himself....
>
> After the meeting I needed to think, and so I started to walk through the heather by myself, trying to understand all I had heard, questioning my own relationship with God.

In a true divine appointment, as she was walking and thinking, she met the Sadhu, who was also out walking, and found him very easy to talk to.

> "Please, Mr. Sadhu, tell me what is wrong with me? I'm a child of God, I have received Jesus as my Savior and I know that my sins are forgiven. I know that He is with me for He has said, 'I am with you always 'til the end of the world.' But what's wrong with me? I've never seen a vision or experienced a miracle."
>
> The Sadhu smiled at me. "Sometimes people come to me to see a miracle. When they come now I'll send them to Corrie ten Boom. That I know Jesus is alive and with me is no miracle... these eyes have seen Him. But you, who have never seen Him, know His presence. Isn't that a miracle of the Holy Spirit? Look in your Bible at what Jesus said to Thomas in John 20:29: '... Blessed are they who did not see, and yet believed.'
>
> "Don't pray for visions; He gives you the assurance of His presence without visions."*

---

* Ten Boom, Corrie, and Carole C. Carlson. 1976 *In My Father's House: The Years before "The Hiding Place."* Old Tappan, N.J.: F. H. Revell Co. pp. 83-84

Reflection

"I am with you always, 'til the end of the world." (Matthew 28:20) Jesus promises that He is with us, and He is, whether we perceive it or not.

Jesus makes His presence known in our lives in so many ways, from answered prayer, to the presence of peace when it doesn't make sense, to a Bible verse that leaps off the page, to a still small voice that maybe we don't even recognize until later.

As Sundar Singh assured Corrie ten Boom, these marks of His presence, and many more, are miracles of the Holy Spirit.

꧁꧂

This story begins on page 33 of the Scripture Testimony Edition of *Sadhu Sundar Singh, A Personal Memoir* from Walking Together Press.

Devotion 23: Pray for Those Who Persecute You

S UNDAR Singh was a round peg in the square hole of the Western, specifically Anglican, interpretation of being a follower of Jesus. That he had the true heart of Jesus, in spite of not fitting into the expectations of many of his most beloved mentors, is illustrated by the following sweet story.

> ...In the year 1909, the Bishop of Lahore, Dr. Lefroy, to whom [Sundar Singh] was very deeply attached, offered to ordain him to the sacred ministry if he would prepare for Holy Orders at the Theological College in Lahore. Out of deference to the Bishop, whom he loved, he accepted the offer of theological training that was made to him and studied under Canons Wood and Wigram in the Divinity School.
>
> But here... he soon found himself out of his element and a stranger among the students, who were being prepared for the ministry. As a Sadhu, his standard of living was quite different from theirs, and his devotional life was also of a different type from the regulated services which were held in the Divinity School. He did not find it at all easy to get on with the students, and for the most part lived in his own small room

apart, meeting them only at meal times and at the stated hours of prayer.

On their side there seems to have been something of the same resentment which he met at [another school]. For the ordinary Divinity students seemed to feel all the while that the Sadhu was setting up a new standard superior to their own, and that they were being silently condemned by his presence among them.

Sundar did his utmost to avoid anything that might be regarded as censorious and remained humbly waiting to win their goodwill and affection; but this did not appear for some time.

One day, a student, who had been a ringleader in this resentful treatment, saw Sundar apart under a tree, sitting alone, and went up quite close to him without being noticed by him. To his great surprise, he found that Sundar was in tears, pouring out his heart to God in earnest supplication on behalf of this very student who had thus come near. He was praying that anything which he himself might have done amiss might be forgiven, and that true love might be established between them.

The student, when he heard this prayer, was so overcome, that he discovered himself to Sundar on the spot and asked his forgiveness, and they became close friends.

Theme

Do not retaliate, instead behave honorably
ROMANS 12:17
Repay no one evil for evil, but give thought to do what is honorable in the sight of all.

Forgiving your persecutor
MATTHEW 5:44
But I say to you, Love your enemies and pray for those who persecute you,

Devotion

I speak from personal experience that it is so easy to resort to righteous indignation when hurt by another. Sadly, this can be especially true between believers, because it's possible that both parties think they are genuinely in the right, trying to live out their respective understandings of the Scriptures. I am ashamed to admit that I have found myself thinking, "Well, I know I'm in the right on this issue. That person will discover the error of their interpretation or practice when their lives fall apart." How horrible! How evil! How dishonorable! How unloving! How unlike my precious Lord Jesus.

What if instead of thinking that Sundar was trying to be "holier than thou," the students had sought to understand him and then asked him how they could help him succeed?

Sundar Singh was unjustly treated by those students that chose to judge him for his different behavior. But instead of returning their evil for the evil of righteous indignation, Sundar obeyed his Lord Jesus, and prayed for his persecutor; that God would help them to love one another.

Reflection

Heavenly Father, give me Your heart. Help me to pray for and truly seek the good of my opponent.

✠

This story begins on page 50 of the Scripture Testimony Edition of *Sadhu Sundar Singh, A Personal Memoir* from Walking Together Press.

Chapter XII

Mimosa

THIS little book tells a highly unusual story. Taking place, as it does, in a turn-of-the-twentieth-century rural Hindu village, and with Amy Carmichael's artful telling, it seems like some kind of tragic fairytale. In fact, at one point the author asks the reader, "Does it read like a story made up, or at least touched up a little?" But it is not a story made up. Carmichael says, "Of all the stories we have touched since we came to India, hardly one has humbled us so much, as we thought of our faithless fears for the little Mimosa. But hardly one has lifted us so high in adoration, and in wonder, and in awe."

Young Mimosa's older sister, Star, was attending the school at Amy Carmichael's Dohnavur Fellowship. One day her father took Mimosa along with him for a visit to the older sister, where they met Amy Carmichael and the other workers in the school. They ate a meal together, for which Star gave thanks to God. They observed some typical afternoon activities, and before her father took her home, the staff prayed a short prayer, committing Mimosa to the love of the Lord.

Mimosa did not return to Dohnavur until she was a grown woman with her own children, and for all that time she never had a relationship with another Christian. And yet, though she came of age, was married, and bore children, as a typical woman in a rural Hindu village, and though she suffered injustice, persecution, privation, sickness, and loss, she had an uncommon depth of faith in the One True God as her *loving Father,* who time and time again answered her prayers and provided for her needs.

How could a little girl who only spent one afternoon in the company of Christians, gain enough light, or glean enough crumbs from under the Master's table, to sustain a profound and effectual faith through her many years of suffering? How could she learn about her loving Father in heaven, whom she asked to gather her and her children under the safety of His wings—like a hen gathers her chicks—without ever hearing or reading (she was illiterate) Luke 13:34? How did she find the conviction and the strength to resist the sometimes violent pressure to participate in the all-pervasive idol-worship of her community? How indeed, except that her loving Father taught her and sustained her.

Mimosa had a child's understanding of God, formed from just a few experiences and chance words throughout her life. Amy Carmichael puts it so well, "We can gather up the less than an infant's fistful of seed corn given to Mimosa. We can count the seeds, they were so few: there were nine. That God is, that He loves, guides, and, being the God of gods, is all-powerful, that He listens when we pray, that as a Father we may think of Him and that "He who plants the tree will water it." That the Place of Release is much better than this world, for there is no pain there, and that the Lord who lived here before will come back. She had also heard that 'some time, at the last,' there would be a judgment and excuses would not stand. But this event felt too remote to find much place in her theology."*

This story is a challenge. What does it mean to walk with God? Is it about having the right information, or about having a relationship with the loving Father in heaven? Of course it's about both. But Mimosa's

---

* Carmichael, Amy. 2023. *Mimosa (Scripture Testimony Edition)*. Estes Park: Walking Together Press. pg. 41

beautiful story is a helpful refocus on the reality and character of our loving Father in Heaven, who is the One to whom all the information points. Perhaps Mimosa's story is unique, or perhaps it is only unique because it has been recorded. Who knows how many other people throughout the world and throughout time have been able to walk with God so intimately without any instruction. Two things are certain, not even one sparrow falls to the ground apart from the loving Heavenly Father (Matthew 10:29), and He is the rewarder of those who seek Him (Hebrews 11:6).

Missionary and prolific author Amy Carmichael worked in South India for the first half of the twentieth century. In addition to evangelism, she ran an orphanage and school, and is most well-known for rescuing children from temple prostitution. Dohnavur Fellowship, as it came to be known, was the refuge for more than one thousand children, and a school to many more, including Mimosa's older sister and brother, and eventually Mimosa's own sons and herself; making her story a *must-read* fairytale in the truest sense, in that she lived happily ever after.

Devotion 24: God Will Complete His Work

MIMOSA had been taken advantage of by her relatives, who essentially stole everything of value she had, leaving her and her family destitute. They had done this partly out of spite because she refused to participate in the Hindu rituals. Her own mother had said, "Let thy God help thee!" In this time of great trial, she cried out to her loving Heavenly Father.

> She had never learned to pray, never heard prayer except when we committed her to the love of the Lord, before we said good-bye....
>
> "O God," she said aloud, and the words seemed to rise through the thin blue air above her, "O God, my husband has deceived me, his brother has deceived me, even my mother has deceived me, but You will not deceive me."
>
> Then she waited a little, looking up, and stretching out her arms: "Yes, they have all deceived me, but I am not offended with You. Whatever You do is good. What should I do without You? You are the Giver of health and strength and will to work. Are not these things better than riches or people's help?" And again she waited a while.

Then, kneeling there in the open field, she drew the loose end of her sāri round, and spread it, holding it open before the Lord. In some such way Ruth must have held her mantle when Boaz poured into it six measures of barley. To the Eastern women it means all that ever can be expressed of humble loving expectation: "For He said, Go not empty." Thus Mimosa knelt: "You will not deceive me."

The sun beat down on her; the little young cotton plants about her drooped their soft green leaves, but she knelt on, heeding nothing, her sāri still spread out before her God: "I am an emptiness for You to fill."

Not one Scripture did she know, there was nothing from the Book of books for the Spirit to take and show to her at that moment. But His resources are limitless, and back to her troubled mind came the memory of a wise word of her father's: *"He who planted the tree will water it."* Yes, God was her heavenly Gardener. Had He not planted His little tree, would He not water it? She dropped her sāri and rose.

Then what happened? ...Suddenly all her weariness passed. She knew herself refreshed, invigorated. He had heard, her God had heard. ...With the little gesture of the folded hands which is the universal Indian Amen, she bowed her head, and stood a moment drinking from the waters of comfort. And then she went to the tree where her baby swung in the light wind, and, taking him from it, threw the wisp of cloth across her shoulders, and walked back to her home filled with a peace that passed her understanding.

Theme

God began a work in you and will bring it to completion
PHILIPPIANS 1:6

being confident of this very thing, that he who began a good work in you will complete it until the day of Jesus Christ.

Don't be anxious, instead make requests known to God
PHILIPPIANS 4:6

> In nothing be anxious, but in everything, by prayer and petition with thanksgiving, let your requests be made known to God. And the peace of God, which surpasses all understanding, will guard your hearts and your thoughts in Christ Jesus. (Philippians 4:6-7)

Devotion

So many books have been written about how to hear from God, and every one that I have read points to the Bible as the primary way to hear God's voice. Indeed, Jesus promised that the Holy Spirit would "bring to your remembrance all the things I have said to you." (John 14:26) With this promise in mind, we read and re-read our Bibles to load His teachings into our minds and hearts, so that at the proper time, the Holy Spirit will bring to mind an appropriate Scripture verse. But this was not the case for Mimosa.

> "Not one Scripture did she know, there was nothing from the Book of books for the Spirit to take and show to her at that moment. But His resources are limitless, and back to her troubled mind came the memory of a wise word of her father's: *'He who planted the tree will water it.'* Yes, God was her heavenly Gardener. Had He not planted His little tree, would He not water it?"

Truth is truth, no matter how it comes to us. A thing is not true because the Bible says it. Rather, the Bible says a thing because it is true. Mimosa's father had said a true thing through which the Holy Spirit was able to bring incomprehensible comfort.

Mimosa, though she lacked the exact words of God's promises, was convinced that whatever He does is good, because He is good. What would she do without Him? This is faith. Truly, there was nothing more to know beyond that.

Reflection

More important than the mere text of God's teachings, is to have faith in who He is, and what He is like.

ॐ

This story begins on page 21 of the Scripture Testimony Edition of *Mimosa* from Walking Together Press.

Devotion 25: Soothing Oil Provided

MEASLES had hit Mimosa's children hard. While all four of her boys recovered, they were still covered with miserable sores and could not sleep at night. Like every other need, Mimosa took this to her loving Heavenly Father.

She was not through her troubles. That treacherous illness had left weakness in its wake. An affection of the skin attacked all four boys, the poor baby was covered with sores and wailed day and night. Lavish anointing with oil would have helped: but the oil bottle was empty, and she could not afford to buy in anything like sufficient quantity.

That was a painful hour. She could have borrowed the oil; but the strange instinct in her uncommunicated by anything ever heard (and, as we know, she could not read), drew her back from borrowing. "Our God knows, and He will give it to us. He will help me to earn more, give me more strength. If it be good for us, this He will do," she said to her little boys.

But that night, as she saw the poor little fellows distressed and crying.... The poor mother pulled herself together.... She went to the little boys, made them kneel on their mats: "Our God can help even in this," she said, and she prayed, prayed for healing, for relief from the unendurable irritation which kept them awake, for help for herself that she might be strong to work and buy what was required, for comfort for them all. Soothed and consoled, the children fell asleep.

But the oil?

Through all these years her sisters had never thought of sending her anything. It was partly, perhaps, that they lived far away and knew little of her struggles, partly, it may be, they knew the temper of her mind and did not care to risk sending an unwelcome gift. She, of course, had never spoken of her difficulties to them; if they knew anything, they heard it from others.

For Mimosa, careful of her God's good name, said nothing to those who would not understand. "I know His love, how could I doubt Him? But if I had told them they would have said, 'Ah, your God is not so good as ours. See, we lack nothing.'"

But now, in their distant town, to the two sisters came a thought of Mimosa and her children, and moved by some kindly, sisterly feeling, they sent twice during that period small, but blessedly welcome gifts. (For so coming who could refuse them?) The oil bottle was filled, and there was enough to buy other necessities of the moment. Cheered and warmed to the heart (but she would have said cooled), Mimosa thanked God and took courage.

And in this way, by prayer and in confidence, this untaught Indian woman dealt with all the emergencies of life, taking sickness, when it came, direct to Him, and looking to Him to heal.

Theme

God answers prayer

JOHN 15:7

> If you remain in me, and my words remain in you, you will ask whatever you desire, and it will be done for you.

According to your faith be it done to you
MATTHEW 9:27-31

> As Jesus passed by from there, two blind men followed him, call-
> ing out and saying, "Have mercy on us, son of David!" When he
> had come into the house, the blind men came to him. Jesus said
> to them, "Do you believe that I am able to do this?" They told
> him, "Yes, Lord." Then he touched their eyes, saying, *"Accord-
> ing to your faith be it done to you."* (Matthew 9:27-29 emphasis
> added)

Devotion

"If it be good for us, this He will do."

Like the three Israelites who defied the king of Babylon and said,
"Even if our God does not deliver us, we will not bow down before
you," Mimosa believed that God would provide for their needs, but
if He did not, that there were good reasons, because God is good.

It was through this implicit trust in God that Mimosa was abiding
in Him, and everything she knew about Him was certainly abiding
in her. So it was according to this faith that she told her boys, "Our
God can help even in this."

According to Mimosa's faith, God stirred the hearts of her sisters
to meet their pressing need.

Reflection

Heavenly Father, increase our faith! May we be able to say with
perfect confidence, "Our God knows, and He will give it to us. He
will help me to earn more, give me more strength. *If it be good for us,
this He will do."*

༄

This story begins on page 91 of the Scripture Testimony Edition of
Mimosa from Walking Together Press.

Walking Together Press is a non-profit publishing
company devoted to supporting grassroots libraries
in Africa through global book sales and through
providing free library editions.

To read our story, to see our catalog, and to learn
more about how you can help us in our mission,
visit our website at:

https://walkingtogether.press

Printed in the USA
CPSIA information can be obtained
at www.ICGtesting.com
CBHW040720211023
1431CB00029B/147